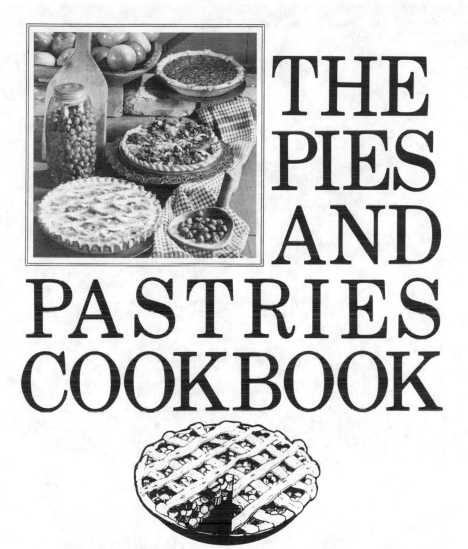

THE PIES AND PASTRIES COOKBOOK

Favorite Recipes® of Home Economics Teachers

© Favorite Recipes Press, A Division of Great American Opportunities Inc. MCMLXXXIV
P. O. Box 1408, Nashville, Tennessee 37202
ISBN 0-87197-167-4

Cover Recipes:
FRENCH CHERRY PUDDING PIE, Recipe on page 30.
CHOCOLATE-ALMOND PUDDING PIE, Recipe on page 33.
PRALINE BUTTER PECAN PIE, Recipe on page 64.

CANDY APPLE PIE, Recipe on page 12. FILBERT CARAMEL PIE, Recipe on page 42.
MINCEMEAT-SOUR CREAM PIE, Recipe on page 51.

DEAR HOMEMAKER:

When you want to bring a smile to the faces of your hungry family, you know to present them with a delicious homemade dessert. Pies and pastries, one of the most popular choices of all, are also one of the desserts by which truly great cooks are known.

That's you! Thanks to Home Economics Teachers, you can master the art of pie and pastry cookery in no time at all. You choose it — cream puffs, chiffon pies, fried pies, tarts, fritters, turnovers, cream pies, or fruit pies — there's a recipe here for all to enjoy!

Sharing time-honored recipes is a favorite pastime of Home Economics Teachers, as their well-known collection of cookbooks prove. And, for this newest cookbook, they've submitted some of their most tempting. You'll reach for it again and again over the years.

Don't wait even one more day to delight your family members with a show-stopper pie or delectable pastry. You can do it with ease using recipes from the Home Economics Teachers' *Pies & Pastries Cookbook!*

Sincerely,

Mary Jane Blount

Mary Jane Blount

BOARD OF ADVISORS

Favorite Recipes Press wants to recognize the following who graciously serve on our Home Economics Teachers' Advisory Board:

MARILYN BUTLER
Vocational Home Economics Teacher
Midwest City, Oklahoma

SANDRA CROUCH
Home Economics Teacher
Sparta, Tennessee

REGINA HAYNES
Home Economics Teacher
Waynesville, North Carolina

KATHERINE JENSEN
Home Economics Teacher
Brigham City, Utah

BRENDA LONG
Home Economics Teacher
Richlands, Virginia

ALMA PAYNE
Home Economics Teacher
Hurst, Texas

SUE SMITH
State Specialist, Home Economics Education
Alabama Department of Education

SHERRY ZIEGLER
Home Economics Teacher
Chillicothe, Ohio

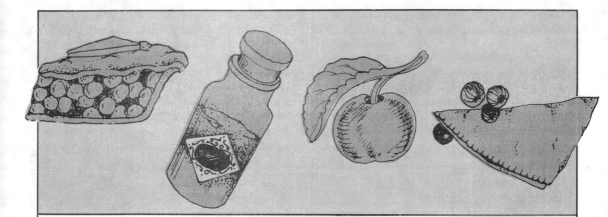

CONTENTS

The Time-Honored "Secrets of Pie

Golden brown. Feather-light and flaky. Tender and melt-in-the-mouth crisp. These are the words used for generations to describe perfect pastry. This quest for excellence is not just a modern concern. Historic records show there were pastry makers in Egypt as early as 3,000 years ago. Pastry making has evolved from the delicacies of the spice-rich Middle East through the adaptations of the trade centers of Spain and Italy into the confections of France and Austria. And, although, all pastries include virtually the same types of ingredients, phyllo, strudel, puff, and short pastries involve differences in preparation, flavorings, and fillings which reflect their national origins.

The importance of pies and pastries in the settling of America is well recorded. Colonial brick ovens were described in terms of how many pies they could hold — there were even 20-pie ovens! Farm cooks would produce as many as 50 to 100 pies at once and serve them at almost every meal. And today, although American cooks still produce the classic pastries of our foreign heritage, pies continue to be our major contribution.

Over the years, the standards for good pie crusts have remained as constant as the basic ingredients — flour, water, and shortening. Achieving a tender and flaky crust is a possibility for every cook! The "secret" is using the right utensils, proper blending, and careful handling. A truly good pie crust results when the shortening and flour are well blended and allowed to melt together quickly in the high heat of the oven to produce flaky layers.

The utensils essential to produce a flaky crust are simple and easy to use. The pastry blender is used to cut the shortening into dry ingredients to achieve the desired "cornmeal" texture. A cloth-covered rolling pin keeps the dough from sticking by releasing small amounts of flour as needed. Too much flour may result in a tough crust. Marble is an excellent work surface because it can be chilled. There are myriad versions of the pie plate — metal, glass, ceramic, decorative, plain, nonstick, and more. A non-shiny surface is best for a golden brown crust. The pastry wheel,

and Pastry Making"

though not essential, lends a finished touch when trimming pie crust edges or cutting lattice strips. A pastry brush is helpful in applying egg white, milk or sugar syrup for a shiny or flavorful glaze. Pie tape or strips of aluminum foil may be used around the edge of the pie crust to prevent overbrowning.

Following proven methods of pastry making is the only real "secret" of perfect results. Be sure to chill all ingredients and measure all accurately. Match the ingredients you have on hand to a specific recipe. Do not substitute a different type of shortening or flour. Use cooking oil only when indicated.

To blend the ingredients properly, sift the measured flour and salt together into a mixing bowl. Then lightly cut in the shortening with a pastry blender until the mixture resembles coarse cornmeal. Sprinkle with cold water, one tablespoon at a time, mixing with a fork in a tossing motion. Enough water has been added when the mixture clings together and the pastry pulls away from the side of the bowl. It should not be damp or sticky. Many cooks prefer to chill the pastry for 4 to 12 hours before rolling out to insure a tender and easy-to-handle pastry that doesn't tend to shrink during baking.

Remove pastry from the refrigerator no more than one hour before rolling out. The "secret" at this point is to handle the pastry carefully. Work on a chilled surface if possible. Softly press the pastry quickly and lightly into a ball. Roll with a rolling pin from the center of the ball outward, never pressing down too hard or rolling toward the center. NEVER REROLL pastry. Instead, patch tears immediately using a bit of pastry and a touch of ice water on your fingertips if necessary.

Roll bottom crust about 1/8 inch thick and two inches larger than the diameter of the pie plate. Fit the pastry into the pie plate, being careful not to stretch the rolled pastry. An easy method of transferring the pastry from the board to the pie plate is to roll the pastry loosely on the rolling pin and then unroll the pastry into the pie plate. Repeat the process for the top crust. Moisten edges with milk or water. Crimp the edges together with a fork or finger for a decorative edge. To create a

lattice top, roll the pastry into a circle two inches larger than the pie plate. Cut the pastry into 1/2-inch strips with a pastry wheel or knife. Weave strips over and under on a stiff sheet of paper or aluminum foil to form a lattice top. Chill for fifteen minutes. Loosen the lattice top from paper with a spatula and slide carefully over the pie filling. Adjust lattice so that it fits onto the rim of the pie shell and crimp edges. Brushing the bottom crust of a juice pie with egg white will help to prevent sogginess while brushing the top or lattice crust with milk and sprinkling with sugar will give a golden crusty finish.

Basic short pastry can be delicately flavored to complement your choice of filling. Use sugar, honey, ginger, cinnamon, or lemon juice for an interesting taste.

For a richer crust, choose a recipe that calls for an egg, cream cheese, or butter. For variety, remember that one recipe for pie pastry is enough to make six or seven 4-inch tart shells, a topping for a deep-dish pie, or four to six turnovers or fried pies.

Cookie, cracker, or bread crumbs may be used to create a delicious crumb crust. And, think of the versatility of gingersnaps, graham crackers, chocolate or vanilla wafers, and lemon crisps in creating an unforgetable crust. It is best to chill a crumb crust thoroughly before filling it so it will not crumble when served. Baking the crust at 375 degrees for five to ten minutes also lends a slightly nutty flavor and crisper texture.

When it comes to pie fillings, there is something for everyone!

FRUIT PIES

In addition to the basic all-American apple, cherry, blueberry, or peach, there are also cranberry, pear, strawberry, rhubarb, plum, blackberry, raspberry, pineapple, and combinations of these. Tangy and delectable, fruit pies (as well as turnovers and fried pies) are usually served warm with ice cream, cheese, or cream.

CREAM PIES

These fillings are pudding-like and may be cooked or uncooked but are not usually baked. Chocolate, lemon, banana, coconut, lime, orange, and cream cheese are favorite flavor choices, but this is by far not a complete list. Cream pies are usually served chilled or even frozen and are great for warm weather.

CUSTARD PIES

These include rich baked fillings based on eggs and butter. Shoofly pie, pecan pie, and chess pie are traditional custard pies, but there are many more! A custard base lends itself to a variety of flavors — rum, sour cream, and spices.

CHIFFON PIES

These pies are elegant with melt-in-the-mouth texture. They are usually made with a gelatin base, and are suited to nearly any flavor — pumpkin, chocolate, coconut, fruits, and many others. Cool and light as air, chiffon pies are a company treat easy enough for every day.

Believe it or not, the pastry that is the basis for *cream puffs* and *eclairs* is one so simple and so versatile it should be a basic part of every cook's talents. Called *chou* pastry, there is no "secret" to making it and rolling it out! The thick paste is merely piped or dropped onto a baking sheet. It rises to several times its original size during baking! They can be filled with whipped cream, custard, ice cream, and so forth for that very elegant dessert! Other speciality pastries include paper-thin strudel or phyllo and light-as-a-cloud puff pastry. For a challenge, you can make the pastry at home. Or buy the pastry at gourmet speciality shops or grocery stores, and create a gourmet confection with little effort.

Now you know the "secrets" of successful pie and pastry cookery. In the sections that follow, pastry makers from all over North America share their tried and true family favorites with you. No "secrets" here — just page after page of mouthwatering pies and delicate pastries for you to share with your family and friends.

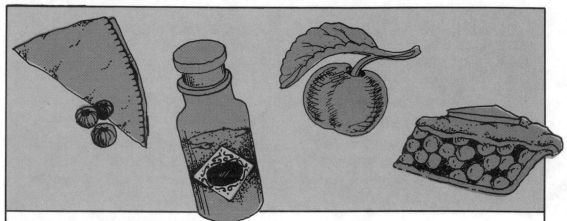

PIE AND PASTRY TERMS

Chiffon pie — A pie whose filling has a light and airy texture as a result of the inclusion of partially set gelatin or gelatin and stiffly beaten egg whites with the other ingredients. This filling is turned into baked crusts of crumbs, plain pastry, or meringue, then chilled to set.

Cream pie — Pie in which a prepared filling is placed in a prepared crust. It is assembled rather than baked.

Cream puffs — Pastries made of a hollow shell or puff prepared with pate a chou (see below), and filled with whipped cream or custard. May also be dusted with confectioners' sugar or iced before serving.

Custard pie — Consists of an egg-based custard filling that is turned into an unbaked pie shell. The entire pie is then baked until the custard is set.

Dumplings — Dessert dumplings feature a fruit center surrounded by dough. When filled, dumpling is dropped into hot liquid and cooked. It may also be baked or steamed.

Fried pies — A fruit or jam filling that is surrounded by pastry and the pie fried in hot fat.

Fritters — From the French *friture,* meaning something fried. A fritter has a fruit center that is dipped in and coated with batter. The pastry is then fried in fat.

Fruit pies — A pie with a fruit-based filling to which either thickened, flavored juice or gelatin has been added. The filling is baked in a shell or between two crusts.

Kuchen — A yeast-based pastry made with cottage cheese, plums, apples, and nuts.

Pate a chou — A sweetened pastry dough prepared by mixing flour, water, seasonings, eggs and butter. The dough is dropped in small amounts onto a baking sheet. As it bakes, it expands, forming hollows that, after baking, may be filled with a sweet mixture, usually whipped cream or custard.

Sopaipilla — A Mexican pastry often served as a hot bread with butter or as a dessert with honey, confectioners' sugar or syrup.

Streusel — A German pastry topped with a crumb-like mixture of butter, sugar, flour and cinnamon.

Tart — A small, open faced pastry consisting of a rich pie shell filled with fruit, jam or custard.

Tassies — Miniature tarts.

Torte — A very rich pastry-like cake made with sugar and eggs and using ground nutmeats, and sometimes bread crumbs, in place of flour. Served iced or with whipped cream.

Turnovers — Small pies made by covering half a piece of plain or puff pastry with a filling, turning the other half over a filling, sealing the edges, and baking the pastry in a hot oven.

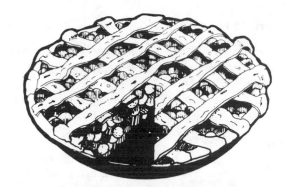

APRICOT-STRAWBERRY PIES, Recipe on page 18.

ALL-AMERICAN PIES

BASIC APPLE PIE

1 recipe 2-crust pie pastry
1/2 c. sugar
2 tbsp. cornstarch
1/2 tsp. cinnamon
1/4 tsp. nutmeg
1/2 tsp. grated lemon rind
6 apples, peeled, sliced
1 tbsp. lemon juice
2 tbsp. margarine

Line 9-inch pie plate with half the pastry, allowing 1-inch overhang. Combine next 5 ingredients in bowl. Add apples; toss to coat. Sprinkle with lemon juice. Turn into pastry-lined pie plate. Dot with margarine. Cover with remaining pastry; seal edge and cut vents. Bake at 425 degrees for 50 minutes or until crust is brown.

Susan Sheffield
Richmond, Virginia

IMPOSSIBLE FRENCH APPLE PIE

6 c. peeled sliced tart apples
1 1/4 tsp. cinnamon
1/4 tsp. nutmeg
1 c. sugar
3/4 c. milk
1 1/2 c. biscuit mix
2 eggs
5 tbsp. butter
1/2 c. chopped nuts
1/3 c. packed brown sugar

Mix apples, cinnamon and nutmeg in bowl. Arrange in greased 10-inch pie plate. Combine sugar, milk, 1/2 cup biscuit mix, eggs and 2 tablespoons softened butter in blender container. Process on High for 15 seconds. Pour over apples. Combine remaining 1 cup biscuit mix, nuts, brown sugar and 3 tablespoons butter in bowl. Mix until crumbly. Sprinkle over apples. Bake at 325 degrees for 55 to 60 minutes or until knife inserted in center comes out clean.

Erline F. Hall
Eastlake, Illinois

CANDY APPLE PIE

7 c. sliced peeled apples
1 1/4 c. sugar
1 tsp. cinnamon
1/8 tsp. nutmeg
1 recipe 2-crust pie pastry
2 1/2 tbsp. butter
3/4 tsp. light corn syrup
1/3 c. toasted filberts, chopped

Mix apples with 3/4 cup sugar and spices in bowl. Spoon into pastry-lined 9-inch pie plate. Dot with 1 tablespoon butter. Roll remaining pastry to 9-inch circle; cut into 6 wedges. Arrange on pie; flute edge. Bake at 400 degrees for 45 minutes or until apples are tender. Cook remaining 1/2 cup sugar in large heavy skillet over medium heat until melted and deep golden brown, stirring constantly. Stir in corn syrup; remove from heat. Mix in remaining 1 1/2 tablespoons butter and filberts. Spoon over pastry wedges on pie.

Photograph for this recipe on page 2.

CHEESE CRUMBLE APPLE PIE

2 c. shredded Cheddar cheese
1 pkg. pie crust mix
3 lb. apples, peeled, sliced
1 tbsp. flour
Freshly grated nutmeg
1/2 c. sugar
1/2 c. packed brown sugar
3/4 tsp. cinnamon
3 tbsp. butter

Mix 1 cup cheese with 1/2 package pie crust mix in bowl. Blend in 2 to 2 1/2 tablespoons water. Roll dough on floured surface to fit 9-inch pie plate. Place in pie plate, making 3/4-inch rim to hold in juices. Arrange apples in pastry. Sprinkle flour over apples. Dust with nutmeg. Mix remaining pie crust mix with sugars and cinnamon in bowl. Cut in butter until crumbly. Layer half the crumb mixture, remaining 1 cup cheese and remaining crumb mixture over apples. Bake at 375 degrees for 40 minutes or until apples are tender.

Nancy Dunn
Williamstown, West Virginia

GLAZED APPLE PIE

2 lb. apples, peeled, sliced
Juice and grated rind of 1 lemon
3 tbsp. sugar
8 tsp. vanilla sugar
1/4 tsp. each cinnamon, ginger
1/4 c. raisins
2 1/2 tsp. cornstarch
1 recipe 2-crust pie pastry
1/2 jar apricot jam
1 c. sifted confectioners' sugar
2 1/2 tbsp. milk

Combine apples, juice, rind, sugars, cinnamon, ginger, raisins and cornstarch in bowl; mix to coat fruit. Pour into pastry-lined 9-inch pie plate. Top with remaining pastry; seal edge and cut vents. Bake at 400 degrees for 40 minutes. Melt jam in small saucepan over low heat; brush over warm pie. Combine confectioners' sugar with milk; blend well. Drizzle glaze over cooled pie.

Marian Liddell
Williamsville, New York

GREEN APPLE PIE

6 c. thinly sliced green apples
1 recipe egg pie pastry (pg. 86)
3/4 c. heavy cream
2 tbsp. flour
2 tbsp. melted butter
1 egg, beaten
1/2 c. sugar
1/2 c. packed brown sugar
1/4 tsp. salt
1 tsp. cinnamon
2 tsp. vanilla extract
Half and half

Arrange apples in pastry-lined 9-inch pie plate. Combine remaining ingredients except half and half in bowl; blend well. Pour over apples. Top with remaining pastry; seal edge and cut vents. Brush with half and half. Bake at 400 degrees for 45 minutes to 1 hour or until crust is brown.

Sharon Glass
Chicago, Illinois

MICROWAVE SOUR CREAM APPLE PIE

1 c. sour cream
3/4 c. sugar
1/4 tsp. salt
1 tsp. vanilla extract
1 egg
Flour
4 c. peeled sliced apples
1 baked 9-in. pie shell
1/2 c. packed brown sugar
3 tbsp. butter

Combine first 5 ingredients with 2 tablespoons flour in bowl. Beat until sugar is dissolved. Fold in apples. Pour into pie shell. Microwave on Medium for 5 minutes. Stir filling gently. Microwave on Low for 10 to 12 minutes or until set. Combine brown sugar and 1/3 cup flour in bowl. Cut in butter until crumbly. Sprinkle over pie. Microwave on Low for 8 to 10 minutes longer or until bubbly.

Leola Down
Lawrence, Kansas

MICROWAVE SUGARLESS APPLE PIE

1 12-oz. can frozen apple juice
*   concentrate*
3 tbsp. Minute tapioca
1/8 tsp. salt
1 tsp. cinnamon
1/2 tsp. nutmeg
2 tbsp. butter
6 to 7 c. peeled sliced apples
1 baked 9-in. pie shell
1/2 c. chopped nuts (opt.)

Place frozen concentrate in 8-inch square glass baking dish. Microwave on High until thawed. Stir in tapioca, salt, cinnamon and nutmeg. Let stand for 10 minutes or longer. Add butter and apples. Microwave, covered, on High for 8 minutes, stirring several times. Microwave, uncovered, for 8 minutes longer or until thickened and bubbly. Let stand for 20 to 30 minutes until cool. Spoon into pie shell. Sprinkle nuts over top. Chill overnight. Serve with whipped cream or ice cream.

Jean Schricker
Grand Rapids, Michigan

PEANUT CRUNCH APPLE PIE

1/2 c. chunky peanut butter
1/4 c. butter, softened
1/2 c. packed light brown sugar
3/4 tsp. salt
1 1/4 c. flour
2 20-oz. cans pie-sliced apples,
  well drained
1 c. sugar
1/2 tsp. nutmeg
1 tsp. cinnamon
1 tbsp. lemon juice
1 unbaked 10-in. pie shell

Combine first 3 ingredients, 1/4 teaspoon salt and 1 cup flour in bowl. Blend with pastry blender until crumbly. Mix apples, sugar, 1/2 teaspoon salt, spices, lemon juice and remaining 1/4 cup flour in bowl. Spoon into pie shell. Sprinkle peanut butter mixture over top. Bake at 400 degrees for 30 minutes.

Marietta Smith
Ft. Smith, Arkansas

SPECIAL SOUR CREAM-APPLE PIE

Flour
Sugar
1/2 tsp. salt
1 egg
1 c. sour cream
1 tsp. vanilla extract
1/4 tsp. nutmeg
2 c. peeled chopped apples
1 unbaked 9-in. pie shell
1 1/4 tsp. cinnamon
1/2 c. butter, softened

Sift 2 tablespoons flour, 3/4 cup sugar and salt into large bowl. Add egg, sour cream, vanilla and nutmeg; beat until smooth. Stir in apples. Spread into pie shell. Bake at 400 degrees for 15 minutes. Reduce temperature to 350 degrees. Bake for 30 minutes longer. Combine 1/3 cup flour, 1/3 cup sugar and cinnamon in bowl; mix well. Cut in butter until crumbly. Sprinkle over pie. Bake for 10 minutes longer.

Dolores Hastings
Edmond, Oklahoma

RED HOT APPLE-PINEAPPLE PIE

5 apples, peeled, sliced
1 8-oz. can pineapple tidbits, drained
1/4 c. red cinnamon candies
1 tsp. grated lemon rind
1/2 c. sugar
2 tbsp. flour
1/8 tsp. salt
1 recipe 2-crust pie pastry
2 tbsp. butter

Combine apples, pineapple, candies, rind, sugar, flour and salt in bowl; mix well. Let stand for several minutes. Spoon into pastry-lined 9-inch pie plate. Dot with butter. Top with remaining pastry, fluting edge and cutting vents in center. Cover edge of pastry with 2-inch foil strip. Bake at 425 degrees for 40 minutes. Remove foil. Bake for 10 minutes longer.

Mary H. Sargent
Minneapolis, Minnesota

TEXAS APPLE PIE

1 recipe 2-crust pie pastry
3 tbsp. butter, softened
1 1/2 c. sugar
1 egg, beaten
1/4 c. pineapple juice
1 tsp. vanilla extract
1/4 tsp. nutmeg
1/4 tsp. each cinnamon, ginger
3 tbsp. flour
3 lg. apples, peeled, sliced
1 tbsp. brown sugar
1 tbsp. evaporated milk

Roll pastry into two 12-inch circles. Fit 1 circle into 9-inch pie plate. Fold remaining pastry in half, cutting slits on fold; set aside. Cream butter and sugar in bowl until light. Beat in egg until fluffy. Stir in juice, vanilla, spices, flour and apples; mix well. Spoon into prepared pie plate. Top with remaining pastry, trimming and sealing edge. Brush with mixture of brown sugar and evaporated milk. Bake at 350 degrees for 1 hour.

Teresa Gray
Smithville, Texas

APPLE-MARMALADE PIE

APPLE-MARMALADE PIE

*7 c. thinly sliced peeled tart
   apples*
3 tbsp. butter
3/4 tsp. cinnamon
3/4 tsp. ginger
1/2 tsp. nutmeg
1 tbsp. lemon juice
*3/4 c. Smucker's orange
   marmalade*
1 recipe 2-crust pie pastry
1 egg yolk

Saute apples in butter with cinnamon, ginger, nutmeg and lemon juice in large skillet until tender. Add marmalade; toss to coat. Spoon into pastry-lined 9-inch pie plate. Roll remaining pastry into 10-inch circle. Cut into ten 1/2-inch wide strips. Brush with egg yolk beaten with 1 teaspoon water. Arrange 5 strips across filling; weave remaining strips in opposite direction to form lattice. Seal ends and flute edge. Bake at 425 degrees for 35 to 40 minutes or until golden. Serve warm.

Photograph for this recipe above.

HONEY-APPLE PIE

6 apples, peeled, thinly sliced
1 recipe 2-crust pie pastry
1/2 tsp. cinnamon
1 tbsp. butter
1/2 c. (or more) honey
2 tbsp. lemon juice

Arrange apple slices in pastry-lined 9-inch pie plate. Sprinkle with cinnamon; dot with butter. Top with remaining pastry; seal edge and cut vents. Bake at 450 degrees for 10 minutes. Reduce temperature to 350 degrees. Bake for 25 to 30 minutes longer or until crust is slightly browned and apples are tender. Remove from oven. Mix honey with lemon juice in bowl. Pour through vents on top crust.

Priscilla West
Franklin, Kentucky

ORANGY APPLE PIE

4 c. peeled sliced apples
1 c. sugar
3 tbsp. flour
1/2 tsp. nutmeg
1/3 c. orange juice
1/3 c. melted butter
1 recipe 2-crust pie pastry

Combine apples with sugar, flour, nutmeg, juice and butter in large bowl. Toss lightly to mix well. Pour into pastry-lined pie plate. Top with strips of remaining pastry. Sprinkle lightly with additional sugar. Bake at 450 degrees for 15 minutes. Reduce temperature to 325 degrees. Bake for 45 minutes longer.

Mary Rogers
Clio, Alabama

ORANGE-APPLESAUCE PIE

4 c. applesauce
Sugar
2 tbsp. grated orange rind
1/4 c. orange juice
2 tbsp. Minute tapioca
1 1/2 c. sifted flour

2 tsp. baking powder
1/2 tsp. salt
1/2 c. shortening
2/3 c. milk
1 1/2 tsp. nutmeg
Melted butter

Combine applesauce with sugar to taste and next 3 ingredients in bowl; mix well. Spoon into 10-inch pie plate. Combine flour, baking powder and salt in bowl. Cut in shortening until crumbly. Stir in enough milk to make soft dough. Shape into 16 balls. Mix 1/3 cup sugar with nutmeg in small bowl. Dip dough balls in melted butter; roll in sugar mixture to coat. Arrange dough balls around edge and in center of applesauce mixture. Bake at 400 degrees for 25 to 30 minutes or until brown. Serve with ice cream.

Verna Larson
Crawfordsville, Georgia

CARAMEL-APPLESAUCE CHIFFON PIE

1/2 lb. vanilla caramels
1 tbsp. butter
1 baked 9-in. pie shell
4 tsp. unflavored gelatin
2 c. canned applesauce
1/4 tsp. salt
2 tbsp. sugar
1 egg, beaten
2 tbsp. lemon juice
1 c. whipping cream, whipped

Melt half the caramels with 2 tablespoons hot water and butter in double boiler over hot water, stirring constantly. Pour into pie shell, spreading to cover bottom. Soften gelatin in 1/4 cup cold water. Melt remaining caramels in 6 tablespoons hot water in double boiler, stirring constantly. Blend in applesauce and gelatin. Stir in salt, sugar and egg. Cook for 5 minutes or until smooth, stirring constantly. Cool until slightly thickened. Blend lemon juice into whipped cream. Whip applesauce mixture until fluffy. Fold in whipped cream. Spoon into pie shell. Chill until firm. Garnish with walnuts.

Wanda Stassler
San Bernardino, California

LIME APPLESAUCE FLUFF PIES

2 1/2 c. applesauce
1 pkg. lime gelatin
1 c. sugar
2 tbsp. lemon juice
1 med. carton whipped topping
2 9-in. graham cracker pie shells

Bring applesauce to a boil in saucepan. Stir in gelatin and sugar until dissolved. Chill until partially set. Blend lemon juice with whipped topping; fold into applesauce mixture. Pour into pie shells. Chill until firm.

Mary Clawson
Flagstaff, Arizona

POPCORN-APPLESAUCE PIE

5 c. popped popcorn
3 egg whites
1 c. sugar
1/2 c. finely chopped nuts
2 c. chunky applesauce
2 c. whipped topping

Place popcorn, 1 cup at a time, in blender container. Process to crush. Beat egg whites until soft peaks form. Add sugar gradually, beating until stiff. Fold in nuts and crushed popcorn. Spread in buttered pie pan. Bake at 350 degrees for 15 minutes. Fold applesauce into whipped topping in bowl. Pour into cooled crust. Chill until serving time.

Ralpha Richie
Oklahoma City, Oklahoma

APRICOT GLACE PIE

1 1-lb. can apricot halves
1 1/2 tbsp. cornstarch
1 8-oz. package cream cheese, softened
1 can sweetened condensed milk
1/3 c. lemon juice
1 tsp. vanilla extract
1 baked 9-in. pie shell

Drain apricots, reserving juice. Add enough water to reserved juice to measure 1 cup. Blend with cornstarch in saucepan. Cook until thick, stirring constantly. Beat cream cheese in bowl until light and fluffy. Add condensed milk gradually; blend well. Blend in lemon juice and vanilla. Pour into pie shell. Arrange apricots over top. Drizzle with cooked mixture. Chill for 2 hours or longer. Garnish with whipped cream.

Barbara Winslow
Fulton, Missouri

DRIED APRICOT PIE

1 1/2 c. chopped dried apricots
1/3 c. sugar
1/4 tsp. salt
2 tbsp. cornstarch
1 8-in. graham cracker pie shell

Cook apricots with 1 1/2 cups water in saucepan until tender. Blend sugar, salt, cornstarch and 3 tablespoons apricot liquid in small bowl; stir into apricots. Cook until thick, stirring constantly; cool. Spoon into pie shell. Chill until serving time.

Carol Lafferty
Monterey, California

DATE-APRICOT PIE

1 c. chopped dates
1 30-oz. can apricots, drained, chopped
1 unbaked 9-in. pie shell
1/2 c. apricot syrup
1/4 c. sugar
2 tbsp. Minute tapioca
1/2 tsp. cinnamon
1 tsp. grated lemon rind
1/2 c. quick-cooking oats
1/2 c. packed brown sugar
1/3 c. flour
1/3 c. melted butter

Arrange dates and apricots in pie shell. Combine apricot syrup with next 4 ingredients in bowl; mix well. Pour into pie shell. Mix oats with remaining ingredients in small bowl. Sprinkle over top. Bake at 400 degrees for 45 minutes. Cover with foil. Bake for 15 minutes longer.

Cindy Warfield
Canton, Ohio

FRESH APRICOT PIES

10 c. sliced fresh apricots
2 tbsp. lemon juice
2 c. sugar
1/4 c. Minute tapioca
1/2 tsp. cinnamon
2 recipes 2-crust pie pastry
2 tbsp. butter
Cream

Combine first 5 ingredients in bowl; mix lightly. Let stand for 15 minutes. Spoon into 2 pastry-lined 9-inch pie plates. Dot each with 1 tablespoon butter. Top each pie with lattice crust. Brush with cream. Bake at 425 degrees for 40 minutes. May prepare filling for freezing by lining 8-inch pie plates with foil extending 5 inches beyond rim. Spoon filling into foil-lined pie plate. Dot with 1 tablespoon butter. Fold foil loosely over top. Freeze until firm. Remove from plate; wrap tightly for storage. Place frozen filling in unbaked pie shell. Top with pastry; brush with cream. Bake at 425 degrees for 60 to 70 minutes.

Brenda Bradford
Portland, Oregon

APRICREAM PIE

1 tbsp. unflavored gelatin
3 eggs, separated
1 c. packed brown sugar
1/2 tsp. salt
1 1/2 c. apricot pulp
1 tbsp. lemon juice
2 tbsp. sugar
1/2 c. heavy cream, whipped
1 baked 9-in. pie shell

Soften gelatin in 1/4 cup cold water. Combine beaten egg yolks, brown sugar, salt, apricot pulp and lemon juice in saucepan. Cook over low heat until thick, stirring constantly. Add gelatin; stir until dissolved. Chill until partially set. Add sugar gradually to beaten egg whites; beat until stiff. Fold egg whites and whipped cream into apricot mixture. Spoon into pie shell. Chill until firm. Garnish with additional whipped cream.

Frances K. Tritschler
Nashville, Tennessee

APRICOT-STRAWBERRY PIES

6 c. sliced fresh California apricots
2 pt. fresh strawberries, halved
4 tsp. lemon juice
1 1/2 c. sugar
6 tbsp. Minute tapioca
1/4 tsp. salt
2 recipes 2-crust pie pastry
Cream

Combine apricots, strawberries and lemon juice in large bowl. Mix sugar, tapioca and salt in small bowl. Stir into fruit. Let stand for 15 minutes. Spoon into 2 pastry-lined 9-inch pie plates. Cut remaining pastry into strips; arrange lattice-fashion on pies. Seal ends and flute edges. Brush strips with cream. Bake at 425 degrees for 40 minutes.

Photograph for this recipe on page 11.

AVOCADO PIE

1 avocado, chopped
2/3 c. lemon juice
1 can sweetened condensed milk
1 graham cracker pie shell

Combine avocado with lemon juice and condensed milk in blender container. Process until smooth. Pour into pie shell. Chill until firm. Garnish with whipped cream.

Sheila Pendel
Lewiston, Idaho

BAKED ALASKA PIE

1 qt. coffee ice cream, softened
1 baked 9-in. pie shell
3 egg whites
1/4 c. sugar
1/4 c. toasted slivered almonds
2 1/4 c. packed brown sugar
1 1/3 c. light corn syrup
1/2 c. butter
1 1/2 c. evaporated milk

Spread ice cream over bottom of pie shell. Beat egg whites until soft peaks form. Add sugar gradually, beating until stiff. Cover ice cream with meringue; seal edge. Sprinkle with almonds. Bake at 450 degrees until lightly browned. Boil brown sugar and syrup in saucepan for 3 minutes. Add butter. Cool slightly. Stir in evaporated milk. Serve warm over pie. Pie may be frozen after baking. Yield: 8 servings.

Jane Latterly
Seattle, Washington

LAYERED BANANA CHIFFON PIE

1 env. unflavored gelatin
1/2 c. sugar
1/4 tsp. cinnamon
1 tsp. instant coffee powder
Dash of salt
3 eggs, separated
1 1/3 c. evaporated milk
1 tsp. vanilla extract
1 baked 9-in. pie shell
2 bananas, sliced

Soften gelatin in 1/4 cup cold water. Combine sugar, cinnamon, coffee powder and salt in double boiler. Add egg yolks and evaporated milk; mix well. Cook until thick, stirring constantly; remove from heat. Stir in gelatin and vanilla. Chill until partially set. Fold stiffly beaten egg whites into gelatin mixture. Spoon half the mixture into pie shell. Arrange bananas on top. Cover with remaining gelatin mixture. Chill for several hours. Serve with whipped cream.

Laura Wood
Spartanburg, South Carolina

BANANA CUSTARD PIE

2 c. milk
4 tbsp. flour
3/4 c. sugar
1/4 tsp. salt
2 eggs, separated
1 tsp. vanilla extract
2 bananas, sliced
1 baked 9-in. pie shell

Combine milk, flour, 1/2 cup sugar, salt and beaten egg yolks in saucepan. Cook until thick, stirring constantly; cool. Stir vanilla into cooked mixture. Arrange bananas in pie shell. Pour custard over bananas. Beat remaining 1/4 cup sugar into stiffly beaten egg whites. Spread over pie, sealing to edge. Bake at 350 degrees until brown.

Diane Centar
Billings, Montana

BANANA CREAM PIE

Sugar
3 tbsp. flour
Pinch of salt
2 eggs, separated
1 c. milk, scalded
3/4 tsp. lemon juice
1/2 c. cream
2 lg. bananas, sliced
1 baked 9-in. pie shell

Combine 1/3 cup sugar, flour and salt in saucepan; mix well. Blend in egg yolks, milk and lemon juice. Cook over medium heat until thick, stirring constantly. Stir in cream; remove from heat. Fold in bananas. Pour into pie shell. Beat egg whites until soft peaks form. Add 1 tablespoon sugar gradually, beating until stiff. Spread over filling, sealing to edge. Bake at 375 degrees for 5 to 7 minutes or until brown.

Barbara Duncan
Parksville, British Columbia, Canada

CARAMELIZED BANANA PIE

1 can sweetened condensed milk
Vanilla wafers
2 lg. bananas, sliced
2 tbsp. lemon juice
1 sm. carton whipped topping
Maraschino cherries

Pour condensed milk into buttered pie plate. Cover plate with foil and place in pan of hot water. Bake at 425 degrees for 1 hour or until thick and caramel colored. Chill until firm. Slip into vanilla wafer-lined pie plate. Arrange bananas over caramel; drizzle with lemon juice. Top with whipped topping and cherries. Chill until serving time.

Susan Denny
Huntsville, Alabama

BANANA-COCONUT CHIFFON PIE

BANANA-COCONUT CHIFFON PIE

1 env. unflavored gelatin
3 eggs, separated
1 c. mashed bananas
1/3 c. sugar
1/4 tsp. salt
1/2 c. whipping cream, whipped
1/3 c. finely grated coconut
1 baked 9-in. pie shell

Soften gelatin in 1/4 cup cold water. Blend beaten egg yolks with bananas, sugar and salt in double boiler. Cook over boiling water until slightly thickened, stirring constantly. Remove from heat; stir in softened gelatin until dissolved. Chill until partially set. Fold stiffly beaten egg whites, whipped cream and coconut into banana mixture. Spoon into pie pastry shell. Chill until firm. Garnish with additional whipped cream and sliced bananas.

Photograph for this recipe above.

DOUBLE-CRUST BANANA PIE

3/4 c. packed light brown sugar
2 tbsp. flour
1/4 tsp. nutmeg
1/8 tsp. salt

1 recipe 2-crust pie pastry
7 med. bananas, sliced
3 tbsp. lemon juice
3 tbsp. butter, sliced
1 egg yolk, beaten

Combine brown sugar, flour, nutmeg and salt in bowl; mix well. Sprinkle 1/4 of the mixture into pastry-lined 9-inch pie plate. Layer bananas, lemon juice, brown sugar mixture and butter alternately in pie plate until all ingredients are used. Top with remaining pastry; seal edge and cut vents. Brush with egg yolk beaten with 1 teaspoon cold water. Bake at 400 degrees for 30 minutes or until golden.

Elva Alden
Albany, New York

SUMMERTIME BANANA PIE

1 1/4 c. vanilla wafer crumbs
1/2 c. finely chopped walnuts
5 tbsp. butter, melted
1 c. milk
1 pkg. vanilla instant pudding mix
1 c. sour cream
2 bananas, sliced

Combine crumbs, walnuts and butter in bowl; mix well. Press into 9-inch pie plate. Combine milk and pudding mix in bowl. Beat for 5 minutes. Fold in sour cream. Arrange bananas in prepared pan. Spoon pudding over bananas. Chill for several hours.

Shirley Mayes
Macon, Georgia

BELLEFONTAINE BLACKBERRY PIE

6 egg whites, at room temperature
1/4 tsp. salt
2 c. sugar
1 tsp. vanilla extract
1 tbsp. vinegar
2 c. blackberries, sweetened, crushed
1 c. whipping cream, whipped

Beat egg whites with salt until stiff peaks form. Add 1 cup sugar gradually, beating until very stiff. Add vanilla and remaining 1 cup sugar gradually, beating until very stiff. Beat in vinegar. Pile meringue into greased 9-inch pie plate. Bake at 275 degrees for 1 hour and 30 minutes.

Increase temperature to 300 degrees. Bake for 30 minutes longer until very lightly browned. Cool. Spoon blackberries into meringue shell. Top with whipped cream. Chill in refrigerator.

Marissa Black
Bellefontaine, Ohio

BLACKBERRY JAM PIE

3 eggs, separated
1 c. sour cream
1/4 c. melted butter
1 c. blackberry jam
1/2 c. sugar
Dash of salt
1 tbsp. cornstarch
1 unbaked 9-in. pie shell
14 marshmallows
1 tbsp. light cream

Combine slightly beaten egg yolks, sour cream, 3 tablespoons butter and jam in bowl; mix well. Add mixture of sugar, salt and cornstarch; mix well. Pour into pie shell. Bake at 425 degrees for 30 minutes. Cool. Melt marshmallows in double boiler. Stir in remaining 1 tablespoon butter and cream. Cool. Fold in stiffly beaten egg whites. Spread over pie, sealing to edge. Bake at 350 degrees for 15 minutes or until browned.

Betty Jo Kimmerly
North Wilkesboro, North Carolina

BLACKBERRY-SOUR CREAM PIE

4 c. fresh blackberries
1 unbaked 9-in. pie shell
Sugar
1 c. sifted flour
1/4 tsp. salt
1 c. sour cream

Place blackberries in pie shell. Sift 1 1/4 cups sugar, flour and salt into sour cream in bowl; mix well. Pour over blackberries. Sprinkle 2 tablespoons sugar over top. Bake at 450 degrees for 10 minutes. Reduce temperature to 350 degrees. Bake for 30 minutes longer. Cool on wire rack.

Jeanette Lower
New Rochelle, New York

LIGHT BLACK BOTTOM PIE

1 env. unflavored gelatin
1 c. sugar
1 tbsp. cornstarch
Dash of salt
2 c. milk
4 eggs, separated
2 sq. unsweetened chocolate, melted
1 tsp. vanilla extract
1 baked pie shell
1 tbsp. rum flavoring
1/8 tsp. cream of tartar
1 c. whipping cream, whipped

Soften gelatin in 1/4 cup cold water. Combine 1/2 cup sugar, cornstarch and salt in saucepan. Stir in milk. Cook over low heat until thick, stirring constantly. Stir a small amount of custard into beaten egg yolks. Add remaining custard slowly, mixing well. Add gelatin, mixing well; strain mixture. Combine 1 cup custard with chocolate and vanilla in small bowl, mixing well. Spoon into pie shell. Chill in refrigerator. Stir flavoring into remaining custard. Cool. Beat egg whites with cream of tartar and remaining 1/2 cup sugar until stiff. Fold into custard. Spoon over chocolate layer. Chill for 2 hours. Top with whipped cream.

Christine Cross
Tulsa, Oklahoma

DOUBLE-CHOCOLATE BLACK BOTTOM PIE

1 env. unflavored gelatin
3/4 c. sugar
1/4 tsp. salt
1 1/2 c. milk
4 eggs, separated
1 tbsp. cornstarch
2 tbsp. rum
1 1/2 oz. unsweetened chocolate, melted
1 9-in. chocolate crumb crust,
   chilled (pg. 89)

Mix gelatin, 1/4 cup sugar and salt in double boiler. Add milk, egg yolks and cornstarch; beat to blend. Cook until thick, stirring constantly. Remove from heat; add rum. Blend chocolate into 1/2 cup cooked mixture. Spoon into crust. Chill remaining cooked mixture until firm. Add

remaining 1/2 cup sugar to softly beaten egg whites gradually, beating until stiff. Fold into gelatin mixture. Spoon over chocolate layer. Chill until firm. Top with whipped cream and shaved semisweet chocolate.

Marilyn Horne
Athens, Georgia

BLACK BOTTOM PEPPERMINT PIE

2 c. sugar
3 tbsp. cocoa
1 stick butter, softened
1/2 c. milk
1 tsp. vanilla extract
1 graham cracker pie shell, chilled
3 c. peppermint ice cream
Whipped cream

Combine sugar, cocoa, butter and milk in saucepan. Cook to soft-ball stage or 234 degrees on candy thermometer; remove from heat. Cool to 110 degrees on candy thermometer. Add vanilla. Beat until fudge loses gloss. Pour into pie shell. Cool. Spread ice cream over fudge layer. Top with whipped cream. Serve immediately. May be frozen. Thaw for several minutes before serving.

Lana J. Crawford
Cleveland, Texas

MICROWAVE BLACK BOTTOM PIE

2 sq. unsweetened chocolate
2 c. half and half, scalded
4 eggs, separated
3/4 c. sugar
3 tbsp. cornstarch
2 tsp. vanilla extract
1 baked 9-in. pie shell
1 env. unflavored gelatin
2 tbsp. milk
2 tsp. rum
1/8 tsp. cream of tartar

Combine chocolate and 1/4 cup water in glass bowl. Microwave on Medium for 1 to 2 minutes or until chocolate is melted; set aside. Beat hot half and half into beaten egg yolks in glass bowl. Blend in mixture of 1/2 cup sugar and cornstarch. Microwave on High for 2 minutes;

stir. Microwave for 2 to 3 minutes longer, stirring every 30 seconds. Stir in vanilla. Blend 1 cup cooked mixture into chocolate. Pour into pie shell. Chill until firm. Soften gelatin in milk. Microwave on High for 15 seconds. Stir into remaining cooked mixture; add rum. Beat egg whites and cream of tartar until frothy. Add remaining 1/4 cup sugar, beating until stiff. Fold into cooked mixture. Spoon over chocolate layer. Chill in refrigerator. Garnish with sweetened whipped cream and chocolate shavings.

Mirella Francis
Little Rock, Arkansas

BLUEBERRY DELIGHT PIES

6 egg whites
1 tsp. cream of tartar
2 c. sugar
2 c. crushed saltine crackers
2 c. chopped nuts
1 12-oz. carton whipped topping
1 can blueberry pie filling

Beat egg whites and cream of tartar in bowl until soft peaks form. Add sugar gradually, beating until stiff. Fold in crackers and nuts. Spread 1/2 inch thick in 2 pie plates. Bake at 325 degrees for 25 minutes or until very lightly browned. Spread cooled crusts with whipped topping. Chill for several hours. Top with pie filling.

Joan W. Harmon
Cochran, Georgia

BLUEBERRY-PINEAPPLE PIES

2 boxes wild raspberry gelatin
1 15-oz. can crushed pineapple
1 can wild blueberries
1 c. chopped black walnuts
2 8-in. graham cracker pie shells
1 lg. carton whipped topping

Dissolve gelatin in 2 cups boiling water in bowl. Drain pineapple and blueberries, reserving juices. Add enough water to combined juices to measure 2 cups. Stir into gelatin. Chill until partially set. Remove 3/4 cup gelatin; set aside.

Add fruits and walnuts to remaining gelatin. Pour into pie shells. Fold whipped topping into reserved gelatin. Spread over fruit layer. Chill for several hours.

Jenny Marshall
Big Rapids, Michigan

BLUEBERRY-PEACH PIES

1 22-oz. can peach pie filling
Juice of 1 lemon
1/2 tsp. mace
1/4 tsp. allspice
2 c. fresh blueberries
2 recipes 2-crust pie pastry

Combine first 5 ingredients in bowl; mix well. Spoon into 2 pastry-lined 8-inch pie plates. Top with lattice crusts. Bake at 400 degrees for 25 to 30 minutes or until brown.

Linette Singer
Stevens Point, Wisconsin

BLUEBERRY CREAM PIE

2 c. milk
1 1/4 c. sugar
6 tbsp. cornstarch
Pinch of salt
1/2 stick margarine
2 egg yolks
1 tsp. vanilla extract
1 baked 9-in. pie shell
1 c. blueberries
1 recipe meringue

Combine 1 3/4 cups milk, 1 cup sugar, 5 tablespoons cornstarch, salt and margarine in double boiler; mix well. Bring to a boil, stirring constantly. Blend 1/4 cup milk and egg yolks in small bowl. Beat egg yolk mixture quickly into boiling mixture. Stir in vanilla. Pour into pie shell. Mix blueberries, 1/4 cup sugar and 1 tablespoon cornstarch in skillet. Cook over high heat until very thick, stirring constantly. Spread over pie. Top with meringue. Bake in hot oven for several minutes until lightly browned. Serve warm.

Joan Newton
Mystic, Connecticut

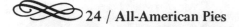

BLUEBERRY-PUMPKIN PIE

BLUEBERRY-PUMPKIN PIE

3 eggs, separated
1 c. sugar
1 1/2 c. mashed cooked pumpkin
1/2 c. milk
1/2 tsp. salt
1/2 tsp. each cinnamon, ginger, nutmeg
1 env. unflavored gelatin
5 tsp. rum flavoring
1/4 tsp. angostura bitters
3 c. dry-pack frozen blueberries
1 baked 9-in. crumb pie shell
1 21-oz. can blueberry pie filling

Combine beaten egg yolks, 1/2 cup sugar, pumpkin, milk, salt and spices in saucepan. Cook over low heat until thick, stirring constantly. Soften gelatin in 1/4 cup cold water; add 2 teaspoons rum flavoring and bitters. Stir gelatin mixture into hot pumpkin mixture until dissolved. Chill until slightly thickened. Beat remaining 1/2 cup sugar gradually into stiffly beaten egg whites. Fold egg whites and 2 cups blueberries into pumpkin mixture. Pour into pie shell. Chill until firm. Mix pie filling, 1 cup blueberries and 1 tablespoon rum flavoring in bowl. Spoon around outer edge of pie. Chill until serving time.

Photograph for this recipe above.

LEMONY BLUEBERRY PIE

4 c. fresh blueberries
3/4 to 1 c. sugar
3 tbsp. flour
1/2 tsp. lemon rind
Dash of salt
1 recipe 2-crust lemon pie pastry (pg. 94)
1 to 2 tsp. lemon juice
1 tbsp. butter

Combine blueberries, sugar, flour, lemon rind and salt in bowl; mix well. Pour into pastry-lined 9-inch pie plate. Drizzle with lemon juice. Dot with butter. Cover with remaining pastry; seal edge and cut vents. Bake at 400 degrees for 30 to 35 minutes or until brown.

Janice Scott
Tombstone, Arizona

SUPER BLUEBERRY PIES

1 c. pecans
1 tsp. flour
1 tsp. sugar
2 unbaked deep-dish pie shells
1 c. confectioners' sugar
1 8-oz. package cream cheese, softened
3 c. whipped topping
2 cans blueberry pie filling

Mix pecans, flour and sugar in bowl. Spread half the mixture in each pie shell. Bake for 8 to 10 minutes or until lightly browned. Cream confectioners' sugar and cream cheese in bowl. Fold in whipped topping. Spoon into pie shells. Top with pie filling. Chill until serving time.

Becky Laughlin
Ocala, Florida

BUTTERMILK MERINGUE PIE

1 1/2 c. sugar
1 tbsp. flour
Pinch of salt
1/2 c. buttermilk
3 egg yolks
3/4 stick butter, melted

1 egg, beaten
1 unbaked pie shell
1 recipe meringue

Combine first 7 ingredients in bowl; mix well. Pour into pie shell. Bake at 300 degrees until set. Top with meringue. Bake until lightly browned.

Louise Bryson
Redwood Falls, Minnesota

BEST BUTTERMILK PIES

2 tbsp. flour
2 c. sugar
1 stick butter, softened
4 eggs
2/3 c. buttermilk
1 tsp. vanilla extract
1 drop of almond extract
Pinch of salt
2 unbaked 9-in. pie shells

Combine flour, sugar and butter in bowl; mix well. Add eggs 1 at a time, beating well after each addition. Add buttermilk, flavorings and salt; mix well. Pour into pie shells. Bake at 325 degrees for 40 minutes. Serve warm or cold.

Marsha Coggins
Harlan, Kentucky

BUTTERSCOTCH PIE

1/3 c. sifted flour
1 c. packed brown sugar
1/4 tsp. salt
3 egg yolks, slightly beaten
4 tbsp. butter
1/2 tsp. vanilla extract
2 c. milk, scalded
1 baked 8-in. pie shell

Combine first 6 ingredients in saucepan. Stir in milk gradually. Cook until thick, stirring constantly. Pour into pie shell. Chill until serving time.

Connie Thurman
Rattan, Oklahoma

CANTALOUPE-ORANGE PIE

4 eggs, separated
1 c. sugar
1/2 tsp. salt
1 tbsp. lemon juice
1 tbsp. grated lemon rind
1 pkg. orange gelatin
1/2 c. orange juice
1/4 tsp. cream of tartar
1 1/2 c. chopped cantaloupe
1 baked 10-in. pie shell
1 c. whipping cream, whipped

Beat egg yolks lightly in double boiler. Add 1/2 cup sugar, salt, lemon juice and rind. Cook until mixture coats spoon, stirring frequently; remove from heat. Dissolve gelatin in boiling orange juice. Stir into egg yolk mixture; cool. Beat egg whites and cream of tartar until stiff; beat in remaining 1/2 cup sugar gradually. Fold in gelatin mixture; add cantaloupe. Spoon into pie shell. Top with whipped cream. Chill for 4 hours or longer.

Belinda Josephs
Covington, Kentucky

CARAMEL CANDY PIE

1 env. unflavored gelatin
28 light caramel candies
3/4 c. milk
1/2 pt. heavy cream, whipped
1 c. chopped nuts
1 tsp. vanilla extract
1 graham cracker pie shell

Soften gelatin in 1/4 cup cold water. Melt candies in milk in double boiler. Dissolve gelatin in hot mixture; cool. Fold in whipped cream, nuts and vanilla. Spoon into pie shell. Chill for several hours.

Francie Holloway
Brevard, North Carolina

CARAMEL CREAM PIES

2 1/4 c. sugar
1/4 c. flour
2 c. milk
5 eggs, separated
1/4 c. butter
1 tsp. vanilla extract
2 baked 9-in. pie shells
1/4 c. slivered toasted almonds

Spread 2 cups sugar in heavy skillet. Cook over low heat until sugar is melted and browned, stirring constantly. Cool slightly. Blend in flour. Stir milk into beaten egg yolks. Blend into sugar in skillet. Cook over low heat until thickened, stirring constantly. Add butter and vanilla. Cool to room temperature. Beat remaining 1/4 cup sugar gradually into softly beaten egg whites, beating until stiff. Pour caramel mixture into pie shells; top with meringue. Sprinkle with almonds. Bake at 350 degrees until meringue is lightly browned.

Cynthia Lansing
Bennington, Vermont

CARROT PIE

6 med. carrots, cooked, pureed
2 eggs, beaten
2 c. milk
1 c. packed brown sugar
1/2 tsp. salt
1/2 tsp. each ginger, allspice
2 tsp. cinnamon
1 unbaked 9-in. pie shell

Combine carrots, eggs, milk, brown sugar and seasonings in mixer bowl. Beat for 2 minutes. Pour into pie shell. Bake at 400 degrees for 15 minutes. Reduce temperature to 350 degrees. Bake for 45 minutes longer.

Sue Forbes
Norfolk, Virginia

CHEESECAKE PIE WITH FRUIT

2   8-oz. packages cream cheese, softened
1 1/2 tsp. grated lemon rind
2/3 c. sugar
1/8 tsp. salt
3 eggs
1 graham cracker pie shell
1 tbsp. cornstarch
1 c. pineapple syrup
1 tbsp. lemon juice

Fresh strawberries and blueberries
Canned pineapple slices and apricot
halves, well drained

Beat cream cheese with lemon rind in mixer bowl until creamy. Add sugar, salt and eggs. Beat at medium speed for 5 minutes. Pour into pie shell. Bake at 350 degrees for 30 minutes. Cool. Combine cornstarch, syrup and lemon juice in saucepan. Cook over low heat until thickened, stirring constantly. Cool slightly. Place 1 large strawberry in center of pie. Arrange strawberry halves around whole strawberry. Surround with blackberries. Arrange 1 1/2-inch pineapple wedges alternately with apricot halves around edge. Spoon cooked mixture over fruit. Chill in refrigerator.

Gwen Clark
Great Falls, Minnesota

CREAM CHEESE PIE

1 8-oz. package cream cheese, softened
2/3 c. sugar
3 eggs
1/2 tsp. almond extract
1/2 pt. sour cream
3 tbsp. sugar
1 tsp. vanilla extract

Combine first 4 ingredients in blender container. Process until well blended. Pour into greased 8-inch pie plate. Bake at 350 degrees for 25 minutes. Cool for 15 minutes. Blend sour cream, sugar and vanilla in bowl. Pour over pie. Bake at 350 degrees for 10 minutes longer.

Bernardine Sullens
Prescott, Arizona

FAVORITE COTTAGE CHEESE PIE

1 1/2 c. cream-style cottage cheese,
sieved
1 tbsp. flour
1/8 tsp. salt
1 c. heavy cream
2/3 c. sugar
Grated rind and juice of 1 lemon
3 eggs, separated
1/3 c. dry currants
1 unbaked 9-in. pie shell
Confectioners' sugar

Blend first 3 ingredients together in bowl. Stir in cream, sugar, lemon rind and juice. Stir in beaten egg yolks and currants. Fold in stiffly beaten egg whites. Pour into pie shell. Bake at 450 degrees for 10 minutes. Reduce temperature to 350 degrees. Bake for 45 minutes longer. Cool. Sprinkle confectioners' sugar over top.

Fran Gillespie
Seattle, Washington

BLACK FOREST CHERRY PIE

1 7-oz. jar marshmallow creme
1 1-oz. square unsweetened chocolate,
melted
1 tsp. vanilla extract
2 tbsp. maraschino cherry juice
1 c. heavy cream, whipped
1/2 c. quartered maraschino cherries
1 8-in. chocolate pie shell

Combine first 3 ingredients in bowl; mix well. Blend in cherry juice until smooth. Fold in whipped cream and cherries. Pour into pie shell. Freeze until firm. Garnish with additional cherries.

Betina Dye
Nowata, Oklahoma

CHERRY-PINEAPPLE-BANANA PIES

1 20-oz. can cherries
1 20-oz. can pineapple tidbits
1/4 tsp. salt
2 1/4 c. sugar
1/2 c. flour
Red food coloring
6 bananas, sliced
1 c. pecans
3 baked 8-in. pie shells

Drain cherries and pineapple, reserving juices. Add enough water to reserved juices to measure 2 cups. Combine with cherries, pineapple, salt, sugar, flour and food coloring in saucepan. Cook until thick, stirring constantly; cool. Fold in bananas and pecans. Pour into pie shells. Garnish with whipped cream.

Jean Roche
Carson City, Nevada

CHERRY MELBA MERINGUE PIE

1   8-oz. jar maraschino cherries
1 tbsp. cornstarch
1/2 c. currant jelly
4 tsp. lemon juice
1/4 tsp. grated lemon rind
4 egg whites
1/2 tsp. vanilla extract
1/4 tsp. salt
1/4 tsp. cream of tartar
1 1/3 c. sugar
8 fresh peach halves, chilled
1 qt. vanilla ice cream

Puree cherries in blender. Blend cornstarch with 1 tablespoon cold water in saucepan. Add cherries, jelly, lemon juice and rind. Cook over medium heat until thick and clear, stirring constantly. Chill in refrigerator. Combine egg whites, vanilla, salt and cream of tartar in large mixer bowl. Beat at high speed until soft peaks form. Add sugar very gradually, beating until stiff. Spread 1/4 inch thick in pie plate, building up side. Bake at 250 degrees for 45 minutes. Turn oven off. Let stand in closed oven for 30 minutes longer. Arrange peach halves in meringue shell. Top with ice cream. Spoon cherry melba sauce over top.

Phoebe Dark
Parker, Arizona

CHERRY PIE SUPREME

2/3 c. sugar
3 tbsp. cornstarch
1/4 tsp. salt
2 c. milk
2 eggs, lightly beaten
2 tbsp. butter
1 tsp. vanilla extract
2 oz. semisweet chocolate, melted
1 baked 8-in. pie shell
1   16-oz. can pitted dark sweet cherries,
    drained
1/2 c. whipping cream, whipped

Blend first 4 ingredients in saucepan. Cook until thick, stirring constantly. Stir a small amount of hot mixture into eggs; stir eggs into hot mixture. Cook for 2 minutes; remove from heat. Blend in butter and vanilla. Add 1/2 cup mixture to melted chocolate; mix well. Spread in pie shell. Cool cooked mixture, covered, for 30 minutes. Cut cherries into halves and reserve several for top. Arrange cut side down over chocolate layer. Spoon cooked mixture over cherries. Top with whipped cream and reserved cherries.

Marnie Kent
Dover, Delaware

EASY CHERRY CHIFFON PIE

1   16-oz. can cherry pie filling
3 tbsp. Brandy
1 carton whipped topping
1 baked 9-in. pie shell

Combine pie filling and Brandy in bowl. Let stand for 30 minutes. Reserve 1 cup topping. Fold remaining topping into pie filling. Spoon into pie shell. Chill until serving time. Garnish with reserved topping.

Amanda Brown
Colfax, Louisiana

CLOUD TOP CHERRY PIE

1 can red tart cherries
3/4 c. sugar
2 tbsp. cornstarch
Lemon juice
Several drops of red food coloring
1   3-oz. package cream cheese, softened
1/2 tsp. almond extract
1 sm. carton whipped topping
1 baked 9-in. pie shell

Drain cherries reserving liquid. Add enough water to reserved liquid to measure 1 cup. Blend with 1/2 cup sugar and cornstarch in saucepan. Cook until thick, stirring constantly. Stir in cherries, 1 teaspoon lemon juice and food coloring; cool. Blend cream cheese with 2 tablespoons lemon juice until smooth. Fold in remaining 1/4 cup sugar, almond flavoring and whipped topping. Spoon cherry mixture into pie shell. Top with cream cheese mixture. Chill for 3 hours. Garnish with toasted slivered almonds.

Missie Leroy
Salina, Kansas

CHERRY PIE ELEGANTE

CHERRY PIE ELEGANTE

2 egg whites
1/2 tsp. vinegar
1/4 tsp. salt
1/3 c. sugar
1 baked pie shell
1 can cherry pie
filling

Beat egg whites with vinegar and salt until foamy. Add sugar gradually, beating until stiff. Spread over bottom and side of pie shell, sealing to edge. Bake for 10 to 12 minutes or until golden brown; cool. Spoon pie filling over meringue. Garnish with whipped cream just before serving.

Photograph for this recipe above.

FRENCH CHERRY PUDDING PIE

1 1/4 c. fine vanilla wafer crumbs
4 tsp. sugar
1/4 c. melted butter
2 c. milk
1 c. sour cream
1/4 tsp. almond extract
1 lg. package French vanilla instant
  pudding mix
1 21-oz. can cherry pie filling

Combine first 3 ingredients in bowl; mix well. Press over bottom and side of 9-inch pie plate. Bake at 375 degrees for 8 minutes. Cool. Blend cold milk, sour cream and flavoring in mixer bowl. Add pudding mix. Beat at low speed for 1 minute. Pour into pie shell. Chill for 2 hours. Spoon pie filling around edge.

Photograph for this recipe on Cover.

FROZEN CHERRY-CHEESE PIE

2 3-oz. packages cream cheese, softened
1/2 c. sugar
Dash of salt
2 eggs, separated
1 tbsp. vanilla extract
1 med. carton whipped topping
1 9-in. graham cracker pie shell
1 can cherry pie filling

Combine first 3 ingredients in bowl; blend well. Beat in egg yolks and vanilla until smooth. Blend in 2 cups whipped topping. Fold in stiffly beaten egg whites. Pour into pie shell. Freeze for 3 to 4 hours. Let stand at room temperature for several minutes before serving. Top with pie filling and remaining whipped topping.

Corliss Spring
Dumas, Texas

SUPER CHERRY PIE

1 1/4 c. sugar
3 tbsp. cornstarch
1/4 tsp. salt
1/4 c. cherry juice
1/2 tsp. red food coloring
1/8 tsp. almond extract
2 cans water-pack cherries, drained

1 tbsp. butter
1 recipe 2-crust pie pastry

Blend first 6 ingredients in saucepan. Cook until thick and clear, stirring constantly. Add cherries. Bring to a boil; remove from heat. Stir in butter; cool. Pour into pastry-lined 9-inch pie plate. Top with lattice crust. Bake at 400 degrees for 40 minutes.

Enid Bagley
Chisholm, Texas

OLD-FASHIONED CHERRY PIE

3 tbsp. flour
3 tbsp. cornstarch
1 1/2 c. sugar
1/2 tsp. salt
3/4 c. cherry juice
2 1-lb. cans pitted sour cherries,
  drained
1 recipe 2-crust pie pastry

Mix flour, cornstarch, sugar and salt in saucepan; stir in cherry liquid. Cook over medium heat until thick, stirring constantly. Stir in cherries. Spoon into pastry-lined pie plate. Top with remaining pastry; seal edge and cut vents. Bake at 425 degrees for 40 to 45 minutes.

Vanessa Delaney
Oxnard, California

SWEET CHERRY PIE

1 1-lb. can pitted dark sweet cherries
1 3-oz. package cherry gelatin
1 pt. vanilla ice cream
1 tsp. lemon juice
3 tbsp. red Burgundy
1 baked 8-in. pie shell

Drain cherries reserving syrup. Add enough water to reserved syrup to measure 1 cup. Bring to a boil in saucepan. Stir in gelatin until dissolved. Add ice cream gradually; stir until melted. Blend in lemon juice and Burgundy. Chill until partially set. Fold in cherries. Spoon into pie shell. Chill until firm. Garnish with whipped cream.

Vicki Barnes
Rye, New York

SOUR CREAM-CHERRY PIE

1 20-oz. can red cherries, drained
1 unbaked 9-in. pie shell
2 egg yolks, beaten
1 c. sugar
2 tbsp. flour
1/8 tsp. salt
1 c. sour cream

Pour cherries into pie shell. Mix egg yolks, sugar, flour, salt and sour cream in bowl. Pour over cherries. Bake at 350 degrees for 40 minutes or until filling is set.

Cassie Winfield
Mount Holly, New Jersey

OLD-FASHIONED CHESS PIE

2 c. sugar
2 tbsp. (heaping) flour
1 tbsp. (heaping) cornmeal
1/2 c. butter, melted
3 eggs, beaten
1/2 c. buttermilk
2 tsp. vanilla extract
1 unbaked 10-in. pie shell

Mix sugar, flour and cornmeal in bowl. Stir in butter, eggs, buttermilk and vanilla; mix well. Pour into pie shell. Bake at 425 degrees for 10 minutes. Reduce temperature to 325 degrees. Bake for 30 minutes longer or until set.

Jean Ellington
Arvada, Oklahoma

LEMON CHESS PIE

2 c. sugar
4 eggs, beaten
1 tbsp. flour
1 tbsp. cornmeal
1/4 c. milk
1/4 c. melted butter
1/4 c. lemon juice
3 tsp. grated lemon rind
1 unbaked 9-in. pie shell

Beat sugar, eggs, flour and cornmeal in bowl until blended. Add next 4 ingredients; mix well. Pour into pie shell. Bake at 400 degrees for 10

minutes. Reduce temperature to 300 degrees. Bake for 30 minutes longer or until set.

Gail M. Skelton
Corinth, Mississippi

CHOCOLATE CHESS PIE

1 c. sugar
3 tbsp. cornmeal
3 tbsp. cocoa
3 eggs, well beaten
1/2 c. melted margarine
1/2 c. light corn syrup
1 tsp. vanilla extract
1 unbaked 9-in. pie shell

Mix sugar, cornmeal and cocoa in bowl. Combine eggs, margarine, corn syrup and vanilla in bowl; mix well. Add to sugar mixture; mix until smooth. Pour into pie shell. Bake at 350 degrees for 45 minutes or until set

Joanne Varner
Cheyenne, Wyoming

MARBLED CHOCOLATE RUM PIE

1 env. unflavored gelatin
1 c. sugar
1/8 tsp. salt
2 eggs, separated
1 c. milk
1/4 c. rum
1 12-oz. package semisweet chocolate chips
1 c. heavy cream
1 tsp. vanilla extract
1 baked 9-in. pie shell

Mix gelatin, 1/4 cup sugar and salt in double boiler. Beat in egg yolks, milk and rum. Cook over boiling water until slightly thickened, stirring constantly; remove from heat. Stir in chocolate until blended. Chill until partially set. Add 1/2 cup sugar gradually to beaten egg whites, beating until stiff. Fold into chocolate mixture. Whip cream with remaining 1/4 cup sugar and vanilla. Spoon vanilla and chocolate mixtures alternately into pie shell until all ingredients are used; swirl to marbleize. Chill until firm.

Clarisse Brown
Boston, Massachusetts

CHOCOLATE-ALMOND SILK PIE

CHOCOLATE-ALMOND SILK PIE

1/2 c. butter, softened
3/4 c. sugar
1 sq. unsweetened chocolate, melted
1 tsp. vanilla extract
2 eggs
3/4 c. chopped toasted almonds
1 baked 8-in. pie shell

Combine butter and sugar in mixer bowl; beat until well blended. Add chocolate, vanilla and 1 egg. Beat at high speed for 5 minutes. Add remaining egg. Beat for 5 minutes longer or until light and fluffy. Stir in almonds. Spoon into pie shell. Chill until serving time. Garnish with whipped cream and additional almonds.

Photograph for this recipe above.

CHOCOLATE-ALMOND PUDDING PIE

1/4 c. melted butter
2 c. flaked coconut
2/3 c. slivered blanched almonds, toasted
1 lg. package chocolate instant pudding
  mix
2 3/4 c. cold milk
1/4 tsp. almond extract
1 c. whipped topping

Mix butter and coconut in bowl. Press over bottom and side of 9-inch pie plate. Bake at 300 degrees for 20 to 30 minutes or until golden. Cool. Chop 1/2 cup almonds. Prepare pudding mix according to package directions for pie using 2 3/4 cups milk. Stir in chopped almonds and flavoring. Pour into pie shell. Chill for 4 hours or longer. Top with whipped topping and remaining slivered almonds.

Photograph for this recipe on Cover.

BROWNIE CRUMB PIE

3 egg whites
Dash of salt
3/4 c. sugar
3/4 c. fine chocolate wafer crumbs
1/2 c. chopped pecans
1/2 tsp. vanilla extract
1/2 pt. sweetened whipping cream, whipped
1 sq. unsweetened chocolate, shaved

Beat egg whites with salt until soft peaks form. Add sugar gradually, beating until stiff. Fold in crumbs, pecans and vanilla. Spread in lightly greased 9-inch pie plate. Bake at 325 degrees for 35 minutes. Cool completely. Spread whipped cream over top. Chill for 3 to 4 hours or until firm. Top with shaved chocolate.

Rhoda Chester
Mason City, Iowa

CHOCOLATE CHIP-WALNUT PIE

2 eggs, beaten
1/2 c. flour
1 c. sugar
1 tsp. vanilla extract
1 stick butter, melted
1 c. chopped walnuts
1 c. chocolate chips
1 unbaked 9-in. pie shell

Combine eggs, flour and sugar in mixer bowl. Beat for 2 minutes. Stir in vanilla, butter, walnuts and chocolate chips. Pour into pie shell. Bake at 325 degrees for 1 hour. Serve warm or cool with whipped cream.

Kathy George
Pittsburgh, Pennsylvania

CHOCOLATE DREAM PIE

2 egg whites
Pinch of cream of tartar
1 tsp. vanilla extract
1/2 c. sugar
1 6-oz. package chocolate chips, melted
1 c. whipping cream, whipped

Beat egg whites with cream of tartar in bowl until foamy. Stir in vanilla. Add sugar gradually, beating until stiff. Spread in 10-inch greased pie pan. Bake at 275 degrees for 45 minutes. Fold chocolate into whipped cream. Pour into cooled meringue shell. Garnish with chopped nuts and coconut. Chill for 4 hours or longer.

Joan Stenger
Norwalk, Connecticut

CHOCOLATE FUDGE PIE

1 1/2 c. sugar
2 tsp. flour
3 tbsp. cocoa
1/2 tsp. salt
1 lg. can evaporated milk
4 egg yolks, beaten
2 tbsp. melted butter
2 tsp. vanilla extract
1 unbaked 9-in. pie shell

Sift first 4 ingredients into bowl. Add milk, egg yolks, butter and vanilla; mix well. Pour into pie shell. Bake at 425 degrees for 10 minutes. Reduce temperature to 325 degrees. Bake for 30 to 35 minutes longer or until firm.

Beth Somerville
Jonesboro, Arkansas

CHOCOLATE MERINGUE CREAM PIE

2 egg yolks
1 tbsp. cornstarch
1 c. milk
1 c. semisweet chocolate chips
1 tbsp. vanilla extract
1 baked Chocolate-Orange Pie Shell (pg. 94)
3 egg whites
6 tbsp. sugar
2 tbsp. pistachio nuts (opt.)

Combine egg yolks, cornstarch and milk in double boiler. Beat until blended. Add chocolate chips. Cook over boiling water until thickened, stirring constantly. Remove from heat. Add vanilla. Pour into pie shell. Beat egg whites until foamy. Add sugar gradually, beating until stiff. Spread over pie filling, sealing to edge. Sprinkle with nuts. Bake at 350 degrees for 10 minutes. Cool.

Carla Leonard
Richardson, Texas

CHOCOLATE-YOGURT PIE

2 c. flaked coconut
1/4 c. butter, melted
1 6-oz. package chocolate pudding and pie filling mix
1 3/4 c. milk
1 carton yogurt
1 c. heavy cream
3 tbsp. confectioners' sugar
1/4 tsp. vanilla extract

Combine coconut and butter in bowl; mix well. Press over bottom and side of 9-inch pie plate. Bake at 325 degrees for 15 to 20 minutes or until lightly browned. Prepare pudding mix according to package directions using 1 3/4 cups milk. Stir in yogurt. Pour into prepared pie plate. Chill for 6 hours or longer. Whip cream in bowl until soft peaks form. Add confectioners' sugar, whipping until stiff. Fold in vanilla. Spread over chocolate layer. Garnish with chocolate curls.

Flora Only
Patterson, New Jersey

FROZEN CHOCOLATE VELVET PIE

1/3 c. butter, softened
1/3 c. packed brown sugar
1 c. graham cracker crumbs
3/4 tsp. cinnamon
1/2 c. sugar
1 6-oz. package semisweet chocolate chips
2 eggs
2 tsp. vanilla extract
1/2 tsp. salt
1 1/2 c. whipping cream, whipped

Combine butter and brown sugar in bowl, beating until creamy. Mix in crumbs and cinnamon. Press over bottom and side of 9-inch pie plate. Bring 1/2 cup water and sugar to a boil in saucepan. Boil for 3 minutes. Add chocolate chips; stir until melted. Combine eggs, vanilla and salt in blender container. Process until smooth. Add chocolate mixture gradually, blending constantly. Fold into whipped cream. Spoon into pie shell. Freeze until firm.

Sandra Larkin
Columbus, Georgia

GERMAN CHOCOLATE PIE

1 4-oz. package German's sweet chocolate
1/4 c. margarine
1 2/3 c. evaporated milk
1 1/2 c. sugar
3 tbsp. cornstarch
1/8 tsp. salt
2 eggs
1 tsp. vanilla extract
1 unbaked 10-in. pie shell
1 1/3 c. flaked coconut
1/2 c. chopped pecans

Melt chocolate and margarine in saucepan over low heat, stirring constantly; remove from heat. Stir in milk gradually. Combine dry ingredients with eggs and vanilla in bowl; mix well. Blend in chocolate mixture. Pour into pie shell. Sprinkle with coconut and pecans. Bake at 375 degrees for 45 minutes. Cool for 4 hours or longer.

Louise Paxton
Blair, Oklahoma

DELUXE CHOCOLATE CREAM PIE

DELUXE CHOCOLATE CREAM PIE

1 env. unflavored
gelatin
1 c. chocolate-flavored
syrup
1 pt. whipping cream,
whipped
1/2 tsp. vanilla extract
1 baked 9-in. pie shell

Soften gelatin in 1/4 cup cold water. Bring chocolate syrup to a boil in saucepan; remove from heat. Stir in gelatin until dissolved. Chill until thickened, stirring occasionally. Fold in whipped cream and flavoring. Spoon into pie shell. Chill until firm. May substitute 1/2 teaspoon almond or rum flavoring, instant coffee powder or cinnamon for vanilla.

Photograph for this recipe above.

BLACK MAGIC CHOCOLATE MERINGUE PIE

1 1/4 c. sugar
3 tbsp. flour
2 tbsp. cocoa
Pinch of salt
2 egg yolks, beaten
1 sm. can evaporated milk
1 stick butter
Vanilla extract to taste
1 baked 9-in. pie shell
1 recipe meringue

Combine first 4 ingredients in saucepan. Blend in 1/4 cup water. Add 3/4 cup water, egg yolks and evaporated milk; mix well. Cook over low heat until hot, stirring constantly. Add butter. Cook until thick, stirring constantly. Stir in vanilla. Pour into pie shell. Spread meringue over filling, sealing to edge. Bake at 350 degrees until light brown.

Francine Alden
Camden, New Jersey

EASY FRENCH CHOCOLATE PIE

1/2 c. margarine, softened
3/4 c. sugar
2 sq. unsweetened chocolate, melted
2 eggs
2 c. whipped topping
1 baked 8-in. pie shell

Cream margarine, sugar and chocolate in bowl for 5 minutes. Add eggs 1 at a time beating for 5 minutes after each addition. Fold in whipped topping. Spoon into pie shell. Chill in refrigerator.

Lela Halliday
Yankton, South Dakota

COMPANY CHOCOLATE-PECAN PIE

Pecans
Butter, softened
1/2 c. dark corn syrup
2 eggs, slightly beaten
1/4 tsp. salt
1 tsp. vanilla extract
1 c. semisweet chocolate chips

Press 3/4 cup finely chopped pecans into buttered 8-inch pie plate. Combine 1 tablespoon butter with next 4 ingredients; mix well. Melt chocolate chips in double boiler over hot water, stirring constantly. Add to egg mixture; mix well. Pour into prepared pie plate. Sprinkle 1/2 cup coarsely chopped pecans over top. Bake at 350 degrees for 25 minutes. Serve with whipped cream.

Wilma Yancy
Bartlesville, Oklahoma

ROYAL CHOCOLATE CHIFFON PIE

1 env. unflavored gelatin
3/4 c. sugar
Pinch of salt
1/4 c. milk
1 egg yolk, beaten
3 sq. unsweetened chocolate
1 tsp. vanilla extract
4 c. whipped cream
1 baked 9-in. crumb pie shell
1/2 sq. unsweetened chocolate, shaved

Mix first 3 ingredients in bowl. Combine milk and egg yolk in double boiler. Add gelatin mixture and chocolate. Cook over boiling water until chocolate melts, stirring constantly. Remove from heat. Beat until smooth. Chill until partially set. Fold chocolate mixture and vanilla into 2 cups whipped cream. Pour into pie shell. Chill until firm. Top with remaining whipped cream and chocolate curls.

Polly Killian
Miami, Florida

MICROWAVE CHOCOLATE PUDDING PIE

1/4 c. butter
1 1/2 c. chocolate cookie crumbs
3 tbsp. sugar
1 sm. package chocolate pudding and pie
    filling mix
2 c. milk
1 c. miniature marshmallows

Microwave butter in 9-inch glass pie plate on High for 30 seconds. Stir in cookie crumbs and sugar. Press over bottom and side. Microwave on High for 2 minutes or until crisp. Combine pudding mix and milk in deep glass casserole. Microwave for 6 minutes or until mixture boils. Cool for 5 minutes. Stir in marshmallows. Pour into prepared crust. Chill until set.

Tina Lumpkin
Ryan, Oklahoma

BROWNIE NUT PIE

1 can sweetened condensed milk
1/4 tsp. salt
1 6-oz. package semisweet chocolate
*   chips*
1 tsp. vanilla extract
2 tbsp. flour
2 eggs, separated
1/2 c. coarsely chopped nuts
2 tbsp. sugar
1 unbaked 9-in. pie shell

Combine condensed milk and salt in saucepan. Bring to a boil; remove from heat. Beat in chocolate, vanilla and flour. Add egg yolks 1 at a time, beating well after each addition. Stir in nuts. Add sugar gradually to stiffly beaten egg whites, beating until very stiff. Fold into chocolate mixture. Pour into pie shell. Bake at 350 degrees for 40 minutes or until firm. Serve with ice cream.

Vera Sanders
Chadron, Nebraska

WHITE CHRISTMAS PIES

1 env. unflavored gelatin
1 c. sugar
4 tbsp. flour
1/2 tsp. salt
1 1/2 c. milk
3/4 tsp. vanilla extract
1/4 tsp. almond extract
1/2 c. whipping cream, whipped
3 egg whites
1/4 tsp. cream of tartar
1 1/2 c. shredded coconut
2 baked 9-in. pie shells

Soften gelatin in 1/4 cup cold water. Combine 1/2 cup sugar, flour and salt in saucepan. Stir in milk. Bring to a boil over low heat, stirring constantly. Boil for 1 minute. Remove from heat. Stir in softened gelatin. Cool until partially set. Pour into large bowl. Beat with rotary beater until smooth. Blend in flavorings. Fold whipped cream into custard. Beat egg whites until soft peaks form. Add cream of tartar and 1/2 cup sugar gradually, beating until stiff. Fold into custard mixture. Fold in 1 cup coconut. Spoon into pie shells. Sprinkle with remaining coconut. Chill for 2 hours or until set.

Wana Miller
Trenton, Texas

COCONUT-BUTTERMILK PIE

3 eggs, beaten
1 1/4 c. sugar
1/4 tsp. salt
1 tsp. vanilla extract
1 stick margarine, melted
1/4 c. buttermilk
1 3 1/2-oz. can flaked coconut
1 unbaked 9-in. pie shell

Combine eggs and sugar in bowl; beat well. Add next 4 ingredients; mix well. Stir in coconut. Pour into pie shell. Bake at 350 degrees for 45 minutes.

Grace Taylor
Nashville, Tennessee

FRENCH COCONUT PIE

2 c. sugar
3 eggs
1 tsp. vanilla extract
1 tbsp. vinegar
1 c. coconut
3/4 stick butter, melted
1 unbaked 8-in. pie shell

Combine first 6 ingredients in bowl; mix well. Pour into pie shell. Bake at 375 degrees until set.

Gay Sheldon
St. Paul, Minnesota

COCONUT-MACADAMIA CHIFFON PIE

1 env. unflavored gelatin
1/2 c. sugar
1/8 tsp. salt
1 1/4 c. milk
3 eggs, separated
1 tsp. vanilla extract
1/2 c. coconut
1/2 c. unsalted macadamia nuts, finely chopped
1 baked 9-in. pie shell
1 c. whipping cream, whipped

Mix first 3 ingredients in double boiler. Beat in milk and egg yolks. Cook over simmering water until thick, stirring constantly. Cool slightly. Stir in vanilla; fold in stiffly beaten egg whites, coconut and nuts. Spoon into pie shell. Spread whipped cream over top. Garnish with additional coconut and nuts. Chill until serving time.

Christine Cross
Cooperstown, New York

IMPOSSIBLE COCONUT PIE

4 eggs
3/4 c. sugar
1 tsp. vanilla extract
1/2 c. baking mix
2 c. milk
2 tbsp. butter
1   8-oz. package cream cheese, softened (opt.)
1 to 1 1/2 c. coconut

Combine all ingredients except coconut in blender container. Process until smooth. Stir in coconut. Pour into 9-inch greased and floured pie plate. Bake at 350 degrees for 45 minutes.

Roberta Charles
Arlington, Virginia

COCONUT CREAM PIE

3/4 c. sugar
Dash of salt
3 tbsp. cornstarch
2 c. milk

3 egg yolks, beaten
1/4 tsp. almond extract
3/4 tsp. vanilla extract
2 tbsp. confectioners' sugar
1 c. whipping cream, whipped
2 c. coconut
1 baked 9-in. pie shell

Combine sugar, salt and cornstarch in heavy saucepan. Stir in milk gradually. Boil for 1 minute or until thick, stirring constantly. Stir a small amount of hot mixture into egg yolks; stir egg yolks into hot mixture. Cook over low heat for 3 minutes, stirring occasionally. Pour into small bowl. Blend in flavorings. Cover surface with waxed paper. Chill for 1 hour or longer. Fold confectioners' sugar into whipped cream. Layer cream filling, half the coconut and whipped cream in pie shell. Top with remaining coconut.

Rosa Black
Sacramento, California

COFFEE-YOGURT CHIFFON PIE

1 env. unflavored gelatin
2/3 c. sugar
3 eggs, separated
3/4 c. milk
1   8-oz. carton coffee yogurt
1 chocolate crumb pie shell (pg. 89)

Combine gelatin, 1/3 cup sugar, beaten egg yolks and milk in saucepan; mix well. Cook over low heat until gelatin dissolves and mixture is thickened, stirring constantly. Cool. Blend in yogurt. Chill until partially set. Add remaining 1/3 cup sugar gradually to softly beaten egg whites, beating until stiff. Fold into gelatin mixture. Spoon into pie shell. Chill until firm.

Judy Evans
Ft. Dodge, Iowa

COFFEE-ALMOND PIE

2 env. unflavored gelatin
2 c. double-strength coffee
2/3 c. sugar
1/2 tsp. nutmeg

3 eggs, separated
1 c. whipping cream, whipped
1 c. salted toasted almonds
1 1/2 tsp. vanilla extract
1 baked 10-in. pie shell

Soften gelatin in 1/2 cup cold water. Combine coffee, sugar and nutmeg in double boiler. Bring to a boil, stirring until sugar dissolves. Stir 3 tablespoons hot mixture into beaten egg yolks; stir egg yolks into hot mixture. Cook over simmering water until thick, stirring constantly. Remove from heat. Stir in gelatin until dissolved. Chill until partially set. Fold in whipped cream, stiffly beaten egg whites, almonds and vanilla. Spoon into pie shell. Chill until firm. Garnish with chocolate curls.

Nola Carpenter
Carmel, California

CRANBERRY-RAISIN PIE

1 1/2 c. sugar
1/4 c. orange juice
1/4 tsp. salt
3 c. cranberries
1 c. raisins
1 tbsp. cornstarch
1 tsp. each grated orange and lemon rind
2 tbsp. butter
1 recipe 2-crust pie pastry

Combine first 3 ingredients with 2 tablespoons water in saucepan. Bring to a boil, stirring constantly. Add cranberries. Cook until berries pop, stirring occasionally. Stir in raisins and cornstarch blended with 2 tablespoons water. Cook until thick, stirring constantly; remove from heat. Stir in rinds and butter. Pour into pastry-lined 9-inch pie plate. Top with remaining pastry; seal edge and cut vents. Bake at 425 degrees for 25 minutes.

Della Mason
El Cajon, California

FROZEN CRANBERRY CREAM PIE

1 8-oz. package cream cheese, softened
1/4 c. sugar
1 pt. vanilla ice cream, softened
1 graham cracker pie shell
1 16-oz. can whole cranberry sauce

Beat cream cheese with sugar in bowl until fluffy. Add ice cream by tablespoonfuls, beating to blend quickly. Pour into pie shell. Stir cranberry sauce. Drop by spoonfuls over ice cream mixture. Freeze, covered, for 4 hours or until firm.

Martha Robinson
Greenville, South Carolina

CRANBERRY-ICE CREAM PIE

1 c. oats
1/2 c. packed brown sugar
1/2 c. grated coconut
1/3 c. butter, melted
1 qt. vanilla ice cream, softened
2 c. fresh cranberries
1 c. sugar

Spread oats in shallow pan. Bake at 350 degrees for 10 minutes. Combine with brown sugar, coconut and butter; mix well. Press over bottom and side of 9-inch pie plate. Chill in refrigerator. Spoon ice cream into crust. Freeze until firm. Cook cranberries in 1/2 cup water in saucepan until cranberries pop. Add sugar. Cool for 10 minutes or until mixture thickens. Spread over ice cream. Freeze until serving time.

Marilyn J. Ziegler
Bloomington, Indiana

CRANBERRY CHIFFON PIE

1 c. sieved cooked cranberries
2/3 c. sugar
4 eggs, separated
1 env. unflavored gelatin
1/2 tsp. salt
1 tbsp. lemon juice
1 baked 9-in. pie shell

Mix cranberries, 1/3 cup sugar and egg yolks in double boiler. Cook over hot water until thick, stirring constantly. Soften gelatin in 1/4 cup cold water in large bowl. Mix in cranberry mixture, salt and lemon juice. Add remaining 1/3 cup sugar gradually to softly beaten egg whites, beating until stiff. Fold into cranberry mixture. Spoon into pie shell. Chill until firm. Garnish with whipped cream.

Barbara Johnson
Youngstown, Ohio

CRANBERRY BAVARIAN PIE

1 env. unflavored gelatin
1/2 c. sugar
Pinch of salt
3 eggs, separated
1 1/4 c. milk
1 tsp. almond extract
1/2 c. whipping cream, whipped
1 baked 9-in. pie shell
1 can whole cranberry sauce
1 tbsp. cornstarch

Soften gelatin in a small amount of cold water. Combine with 1/4 cup sugar and salt in bowl. Beat egg yolks in double boiler. Stir in milk and gelatin mixture. Cook over hot water until mixture coats spoon, stirring constantly. Stir in flavoring. Chill until partially set, stirring occasionally. Beat until smooth. Beat egg whites in bowl until soft peaks form. Add 1/4 cup sugar gradually, beating until stiff. Fold in custard and whipped cream. Pour into pie shell. Chill until set. Cook cranberry sauce with cornstarch in saucepan until clear and thick, stirring constantly. Cool. Spread over gelatin layer. Chill until serving time.

Ardys Robbins
Bluejacket, Oklahoma

FRENCH CURRANT CREAM PIE

1 c. currants
1 c. sugar
1 tbsp. flour
1 c. sour cream
2 eggs, separated
1/2 tsp. cinnamon
1 tsp. soda
1/4 tsp. salt
1 baked 9-in. pie shell
1/4 tsp. cream of tartar

Mix currants, 3/4 cup sugar and flour in 2-quart saucepan. Add sour cream, beaten egg yolks, cinnamon, soda and salt. Cook over medium heat until thick, stirring occasionally. Pour into pie shell. Beat egg whites until frothy; add cream of tartar and remaining 1/4 cup sugar. Beat until stiff. Spread over pie, sealing to edge. Bake at 425 degrees for 5 minutes.

Merrilee Bond
Cedar City, Utah

CURRANT-WALNUT PIES

1   11-oz. box currants
2 eggs, beaten
1 tbsp. butter
2 c. packed brown sugar
1 tsp. vanilla extract
1 c. chopped walnuts
2 unbaked pie shells

Cover currants with boiling water in bowl. Let stand for several minutes; drain. Add eggs, butter, brown sugar, vanilla and walnuts; mix well. Spoon into pie shells. Bake at 350 degrees for 30 minutes. Serve warm garnished with whipped topping.

Clara Josten
Hobbs, New Mexico

MICROWAVE CREME DE MENTHE PIE

30 marshmallows
1/2 c. milk
2 c. chocolate wafer crumbs
2 tbsp. sugar
6 tbsp. margarine
1/4 to 1/2 c. Creme de Menthe
2 or 3 drops of mint flavoring
1/2 pt. whipping cream, whipped

Place marshmallows and milk in 2-quart glass casserole. Microwave on High until melted; blend well. Chill until partially set. Combine crumbs, sugar and margarine in 9-inch glass pie plate. Microwave on High until margarine melts; mix well. Press over bottom and side of pie plate. Microwave on High for 1 minute and 30 seconds. Stir Creme de Menthe and flavoring into marshmallow mixture. Fold in whipped cream. Pour into cooled crust. Chill for several hours.

Frances Kucera
Eugene, Oregon

FRENCH VANILLA CUSTARD PIE

4 eggs, beaten
1/2 c. sugar
1/4 tsp. salt
1/2 tsp. vanilla extract

2 1/2 c. milk, scalded
1 unbaked pie shell
Nutmeg

Blend first 4 ingredients in bowl. Stir in hot milk gradually. Pour into pie shell. Sprinkle with nutmeg. Bake at 350 degrees for 40 minutes or until custard tests done. Cool on rack. Chill until serving time.

Virginia Hoobler
Chamblee, Georgia

DATE CHIFFON PIE

1 env. unflavored gelatin
1/2 c. sugar
2 eggs, separated
1/2 c. orange juice
1/3 c. lemon juice
1/2 c. light cream
Pinch of salt
2/3 c. chopped dates
1 baked 8-in. pie shell

Mix gelatin and 1/4 cup sugar in saucepan. Beat egg yolks, orange juice and lemon juice in bowl. Stir into gelatin mixture. Cook over low heat until gelatin dissolves and mixture thickens, stirring constantly. Cool. Stir in cream. Beat egg whites with salt until soft peaks form. Add remaining 1/4 cup sugar; beat until stiff. Fold into custard. Fold in dates. Spoon into pie shell. Chill for 3 hours or longer.

Jamie Gore
New London, Connecticut

EGGNOG CHIFFON PIE

1 env. unflavored gelatin
1 1/2 c. milk, scalded
Sugar
1/2 tsp. salt
4 egg yolks, beaten
1 c. whipping cream
1 tsp. nutmeg
2 egg whites
2 tbsp. rum
2 tsp. vanilla extract
1 baked 10-in. pie shell

Soften gelatin in 1/4 cup cold water. Combine milk, 5 tablespoons sugar and salt in double boiler. Heat over simmering water until scalded. Stir 3 tablespoons hot mixture into egg yolks; stir egg yolks into hot mixture. Cook until thick, stirring constantly. Stir in gelatin until dissolved. Chill until partially set. Beat whipping cream until soft peaks form. Beat 1/4 cup sugar and 1/2 teaspoon nutmeg gradually into softly beaten egg whites, beating until stiff. Fold whipped cream, egg whites, rum and vanilla into gelatin mixture. Spoon into pie shell. Sprinkle with 1/2 teaspoon nutmeg. Chill until firm.

Anita King
Crossfield, Wisconsin

EGGNOG-RICE PIE

3 c. cooked rice
1 qt. eggnog
1 tbsp. unflavored gelatin
3 tbsp. cream Sherry
1 10-in. chocolate cookie crumb pie shell
1/3 c. crushed peppermint candy
1 carton whipped topping

Cook rice in eggnog for 20 to 25 minutes or until creamy but not too thick. Soften gelatin in 2 tablespoons cold water. Stir into hot rice mixture until gelatin is dissolved. Add Sherry. Cool. Turn into pie shell. Chill in refrigerator. Fold peppermint candy into whipped topping. Swirl on top of pie.

Pat Linz
Sheridan, Wyoming

FRUIT COCKTAIL PIES

1 lg. container whipped topping
1 can sweetened condensed milk
1/4 c. lemon juice
1 29-oz. can fruit cocktail, drained
1 sm. can crushed pineapple, drained
2 8-in. graham cracker pie shells

Combine first 3 ingredients in bowl; blend well. Fold in fruit. Spoon into pie shells. Chill for several hours.

Lin Freeman
Lafayette, Indiana

FRESH FIG PIE

2 env. unflavored gelatin
2 eggs, separated
6 tbsp. sugar
1/8 tsp. salt
3/4 c. milk, scalded
1 tbsp. grated orange rind
2 tbsp. orange liqueur
2 c. chopped ripe figs
1/2 c. heavy cream, whipped
1 9-in. graham cracker pie shell

Soften gelatin in 1/4 cup cold water. Beat egg yolks with 4 tablespoons sugar and salt in small bowl. Stir a small amount of hot milk into egg yolks; stir egg yolks into hot milk. Cook over low heat until thick, stirring constantly. Stir in gelatin until dissolved; remove from heat. Stir in rind and liqueur. Cool until partially set. Beat egg whites with remaining 2 tablespoons sugar until stiff. Fold figs, egg whites and whipped cream into cooked mixture. Spoon into pie shell. Chill until set.

Amy French
Blue Rapids, Minnesota

FILBERT CARAMEL PIE

3 eggs
1/2 c. packed dark brown sugar
1 c. light corn syrup
1/4 tsp. salt
1 tsp. vanilla extract
1/2 c. butter, melted
1 1/2 c. coarsely chopped toasted filberts
1 unbaked 9-in. pie shell

Combine first 5 ingredients in mixer bowl; beat until smooth. Stir in butter and filberts. Pour into pie shell. Bake at 375 degrees for 45 minutes or until set.

Variation: Beat 4 ounces softened cream cheese with 1 egg and 2 tablespoons milk until smooth. Pour into pie shell. Top with caramel mixture prepared above and bake as directed.

Photograph for this recipe on page 2.

PURPLE PASSION PIE

1 tsp. gelatin
4 eggs, separated

1/2 c. lemon juice
1/4 tsp. salt
1 6-oz. can frozen grape juice
    concentrate, thawed
1/2 c. sugar
2 or 3 drops of red food coloring
Dash of cinnamon
1 baked 9-in. pie shell
Sweetened whipped cream
1/4 tsp. almond extract

Soften gelatin in 1/2 cup cold water. Combine well-beaten egg yolks, lemon juice and salt in double boiler. Add grape juice mixed with enough water to measure 1 cup; mix well. Cook over hot water for 10 minutes or until mixture coats spoon, stirring frequently. Stir in gelatin until dissolved. Let stand for 10 minutes. Beat sugar into stiffly beaten egg whites. Tint with food coloring. Fold in cinnamon. Fold into grape juice mixture. Chill for 1 hour. Pour into pie shell. Chill for 4 hours. Top with whipped cream flavored with almond extract.

Jodi Mills
Trenton, New Jersey

CONCORD GRAPE PIE

1 1/2 qt. Concord grapes
1 1/2 c. sugar
3 tbsp. Minute tapioca
1 tsp. butter
1/8 tsp. salt
1/2 c. chopped pecans
1 recipe 2-crust pie pastry

Slip grape skins from pulp, reserving skins. Bring pulp to a simmer in saucepan. Put through sieve to remove seeds. Add enough pulp to reserved skins to measure 3 1/2 cups. Mix grape mixture with sugar, tapioca, butter, salt and pecans. Spoon into pastry-lined 9-inch pie plate. Top with remaining pastry; seal edge and cut vents. Bake at 425 degrees for 15 minutes. Reduce temperature to 400 degrees. Bake for 30 minutes longer.

Zelda Frampton
Titusville, Pennsylvania

GRAPEFRUIT JUICE PIE

1 1/4 c. grapefruit juice
1 1/4 c. sugar

3 tbsp. cornstarch
2 eggs, separated
1 baked 9-in. pie shell
1/4 tsp. salt

Combine 1 cup grapefruit juice, 1/2 cup water and 1 cup sugar in saucepan. Bring to a boil. Combine cornstarch and remaining grapefruit juice. Stir into hot mixture. Cook until thick, stirring constantly. Stir a small amount of hot mixture into beaten egg yolks; stir egg yolks into hot mixture. Pour into pie shell. Beat egg whites with salt and remaining 1/4 cup sugar until stiff. Spread over filling; seal to edge. Bake at 350 degrees for 15 minutes or until brown.

Jenny Brewer
Ely, Nevada

PINK GRAPEFRUIT PARFAIT PIE

1 env. unflavored gelatin
1/2 c. pink grapefruit juice
1 pt. vanilla ice cream, softened
2 egg whites
1 tbsp. sugar
2 c. pink grapefruit sections, chopped
1 baked 9-in. pie shell

Combine gelatin and juice in small saucepan. Let stand for 1 minute. Cook over low heat until gelatin dissolves, stirring constantly. Remove from heat. Stir in ice cream. Chill until thick, stirring occasionally. Beat egg whites in medium bowl until soft peaks form. Add sugar gradually, beating until stiff. Fold into gelatin mixture. Fold in grapefruit. Pour into pie shell. Chill until firm. Garnish with whipped cream and additional grapefruit sections.

Julie Wilkes
Vincennes, Indiana

GRASSHOPPER PIE

32 lg. marshmallows
1/2 c. milk
1/4 c. Creme de Menthe
3 tbsp. white Creme de Cacao
1 1/2 c. whipping cream, whipped
Several drops of green food coloring (opt.)
1   9-in. chocolate crumb pie shell (pg. 89)

Combine marshmallows and milk in saucepan. Cook over medium heat until marshmallows melt, stirring constantly. Chill until thickened. Blend in liqueurs. Fold whipped cream and food coloring into marshmallow mixture. Pour into pie shell. Freeze until firm. Garnish with grated chocolate.

Betty Baker
Columbia, Tennessee

MICROWAVE HONEY-YOGURT PIE

1 c. oats
1/3 c. finely chopped nuts
2 tbsp. brown sugar
3 to 4 tbsp. butter, melted
1/2 tsp. cinnamon
4 1/2 tsp. unflavored gelatin
3 c. lemon yogurt
1/4 c. honey
1 1/2 c. heavy cream, whipped

Combine first 5 ingredients in bowl; mix well. Press over bottom and side of oiled 9-inch pie plate. Microwave on High for 3 to 4 minutes. Cool. Soften gelatin in 1/2 cup water in glass bowl. Microwave on High for 1 to 2 minutes or until dissolved. Blend yogurt and honey in bowl. Stir in gelatin gradually. Chill until slightly thickened. Fold in whipped cream. Chill until slightly thickened. Pour into pie shell. Chill until firm.

Mary Lukan
Boron, California

KIWI PIE

1 jar marshmallow creme
2 tbsp. Creme de Menthe
1 c. whipping cream, whipped
1   9-in. chocolate crumb pie shell (pg. 89)
2 kiwi fruit, peeled, thinly sliced

Blend marshmallow creme and Creme de Menthe in bowl. Fold in whipped cream. Spread in pie shell. Arrange kiwi slices over top. Chill until serving time.

Martine Gabler
Salem, Oregon

JEFF DAVIS PIES

3 c. sugar
1/2 c. butter, softened
1 tbsp. flour
1/2 tsp. salt
1 tsp. vanilla extract
4 eggs, slightly beaten
1 c. milk
1 recipe 2-crust pie pastry

Cream sugar and butter in bowl. Blend in flour, salt and vanilla. Add eggs to creamed mixture. Add milk gradually, stirring until smooth. Line two 9-inch pie pans with pastry. Pour in filling. Bake at 275 degrees for 1 hour or until firm and golden brown. Serve slightly warm.

Essie Stanley
Satillo, Texas

LEMON CHEESECAKE PIE

2 c. cottage cheese
2 packages lemon instant pudding mix
1 3/4 c. milk
2 tbsp. grated lemon rind
1 9-in. Coconut-Pecan Pie Shell (pg. 92)
1/2 c. sour cream
1/4 c. chopped pecans

Beat cottage cheese in bowl until smooth. Prepare pudding mix according to package directions using 1 3/4 cups milk. Combine pudding, cottage cheese and lemon rind; blend well. Spoon into pie shell. Top with sour cream and pecans. Chill for several hours.

Lollie Haron
Upper Sandusky, Ohio

LEMON ICEBOX PIE

1 1/2 c. vanilla wafer crumbs
1/2 c. melted butter
16 (about) vanilla wafers
1 can sweetened condensed milk
3 eggs, separated
1/2 c. lemon juice
1/3 c. sugar
1 tsp. vanilla extract

Combine crumbs and butter in bowl; mix well. Spread in bottom of 9-inch pie plate. Stand whole wafers on edge around plate. Blend condensed milk and beaten egg yolks in bowl. Add lemon juice gradually, blending well. Pour into prepared pie plate. Add sugar and vanilla gradually to stiffly beaten egg whites, beating constantly. Spread over filling. Bake at 350 degrees until brown. Chill until serving time.

Paige Smith
Wilmington, Delaware

LEMON DAIQUIRI PIE

1 sm. package lemon pudding and pie
*   filling mix*
1 sm. package lime gelatin
1/3 c. sugar
2 eggs, slightly beaten
1/2 c. rum
2 c. whipped topping
1 baked 9-in. graham cracker pie shell

Combine first 3 ingredients with 1/4 cup water and eggs in saucepan; mix well. Blend in 2 1/4 cups water. Bring to a boil over medium heat, stirring constantly. Stir in rum. Chill for 1 1/2 hours. Fold in whipped topping. Spoon into pie shell. Chill for 2 hours or until firm. Garnish with additional whipped topping and lemon slices.

Carol Johnson
Leadville, Colorado

LUSCIOUS LEMON PIE

1 c. sugar
3 tbsp. cornstarch
1 tbsp. lemon rind
1/4 c. butter
1/4 c. lemon juice
1 c. milk
3 egg yolks, slightly beaten
1 c. sour cream
1 baked 9-in. pie shell

Combine first 7 ingredients in heavy saucepan. Cook over medium heat until smooth and thick, stirring constantly. Cool, covered, to room temperature. Fold in sour cream. Pour into pie shell. Chill for 2 hours or longer.

Naomi Mayes
Bowling Green, Kentucky

LEMON CREAM PIE

MARVELOUS LEMON MERINGUE PIE

1 1/2 c. sugar
1/3 c. cornstarch
1/4 tsp. salt
4 eggs, separated
2 tbsp. butter
1   6-oz. can frozen lemonade concentrate, thawed
1 baked 9-in. pie shell
1/4 tsp. cream of tartar

Combine 1 cup sugar, cornstarch and salt in saucepan; mix well. Stir in 1 1/2 cups hot water gradually. Mix in slightly beaten egg yolks, butter and lemonade. Bring to a boil over low heat, stirring constantly. Boil for 1 minute, stirring constantly. Cool to lukewarm. Spread in pie shell. Beat egg whites with cream of tartar until soft peaks form. Add remaining 1/2 cup sugar 1 tablespoon at a time, beating until stiff. Spread over filling; seal to edge. Bake at 325 degrees for 20 to 25 minutes or until lightly browned.

Ann Dever
Wilkesboro, North Carolina

LEMON CREAM PIE

1/2 c. cornstarch
1 1/4 c. sugar
1/8 tsp. salt
2 c. milk, scalded
3 eggs, separated
Lemon juice
1 tsp. grated lemon rind
2 tbsp. butter
1 baked 9-in. pie shell

Mix cornstarch, 1 cup sugar and salt in double boiler. Blend in milk gradually. Cook until thick, stirring constantly. Stir a small amount of hot mixture into beaten egg yolks; stir egg yolks into hot mixture. Cook for 2 minutes longer; remove from heat. Stir in 1/3 cup lemon juice, rind and butter. Cool. Fold in 1 stiffly beaten egg white. Pour into pie shell. Beat 2 egg whites with 1 teaspoon lemon juice until frothy. Add 1/4 cup sugar gradually, beating until stiff. Spread over filling; seal to edge. Bake at 350 degrees for 15 minutes or until lightly browned.

Photograph for this recipe above.

BEST-EVER LEMON PIE

Sugar
7 tbsp. cornstarch
3 eggs, separated
1/3 c. lemon juice
3 tbsp. butter
1 1/2 tsp. lemon extract
2 tsp. vinegar
1 baked 9-in. pie shell
Pinch of salt
1 tsp. vanilla extract

Combine 1 1/4 cups sugar and 6 tablespoons cornstarch in double boiler. Blend in 2 cups water. Beat egg yolks and lemon juice together. Stir into sugar mixture. Cook over boiling water for 25 minutes or until thick, stirring constantly. Stir in butter, lemon extract and vinegar. Pour into pie shell. Blend 1 tablespoon cornstarch with 2 tablespoons cold water in saucepan. Add 1/2 cup boiling water. Cook until thick and clear, stirring constantly. Let stand until completely cool. Beat egg whites until foamy. Add 6 tablespoons sugar, beating until stiff. Mix in salt and vanilla. Beat in cold cornstarch mixture gradually. Spread over pie filling. Bake at 350 degrees for 10 minutes.

Kay Caskey
Reno, Nevada

LEMON PIE A LA MODE

1/2 c. butter, melted
2 tsp. grated lemon rind
1/3 c. lemon juice
1/2 tsp. salt
1 1/2 c. sugar
5 eggs
1 qt. vanilla ice cream, softened
1 baked 10-in. pie shell

Combine butter, lemon rind, lemon juice, salt and 1 cup sugar in double boiler. Separate 3 eggs. Beat 2 whole eggs and 3 egg yolks in bowl. Stir into lemon mixture. Cook until thick and smooth, stirring constantly. Chill in refrigerator. Spoon half the ice cream into pie shell. Spread half the lemon mixture on top. Freeze until firm. Repeat layers with remaining ice cream and lemon mixture. Beat 3 egg whites in

bowl until soft peaks form. Add remaining 1/2 cup sugar gradually, beating until stiff. Spread over pie; seal tightly to crust. Bake at 475 degrees for 3 minutes or until lightly browned. Freeze until serving time.

Edith G. Gray
Salt Lake City, Utah

LEMON ANGEL PIE

4 eggs, separated
1 1/4 c. sugar
Salt
1/4 tsp. cream of tartar
1 tbsp. grated lemon rind
3 tbsp. lemon juice
1 c. heavy cream, whipped

Combine egg whites, 3/4 cup sugar, 1/4 teaspoon salt and cream of tartar in bowl; beat until stiff. Spread in buttered 9-inch pie plate. Place in preheated 450-degree oven; turn oven off. Let stand in closed oven for 5 hours or longer. Beat egg yolks in double boiler until thick. Add remaining 1/2 cup sugar, dash of salt, lemon rind and juice; beat well. Cook for 5 minutes or until thick, stirring constantly. Spread half the whipped cream in shell. Spoon cooled filling on top. Top with remaining whipped cream. Chill for 5 hours or longer.

Tamara Dobson
Pierre, South Dakota

LEMON SPONGE PIE

3 tbsp. butter, softened
1 1/4 c. sugar
4 eggs, separated
3 tbsp. flour
1 1/4 c. milk
2 tbsp. grated lemon rind
1/3 c. lemon juice
Dash of salt
1 unbaked 10-in. pie shell

Cream butter and sugar in bowl. Add egg yolks, flour, milk, rind, juice and salt. Beat until smooth. Fold in stiffly beaten egg whites. Pour into pie shell. Bake at 375 degrees for 15 minutes. Reduce temperature to 300 degrees. Bake for 45 to 50 minutes longer.

Janet M. Filer
Arlington, Virginia

PEANUTTY LEMONADE PIE

7 oz. sweetened condensed milk
3 oz. frozen lemonade concentrate, thawed
Peanut butter
1 9-oz. carton whipped topping
1 unbaked 9-in. graham cracker pie shell
1/3 c. margarine
2 1/2 c. quick-cooking oats
1/2 c. packed brown sugar
1/2 c. finely chopped peanuts

Mix first 2 ingredients with 1/2 cup peanut butter in bowl. Stir in whipped topping. Spoon into pie shell. Melt 1/3 cup peanut butter and margarine over low heat in saucepan, stirring occasionally. Add remaining ingredients; mix well. Spread in jelly roll pan. Bake at 350 degrees for 15 to 18 minutes or until golden brown, stirring occasionally. Sprinkle cooled topping over lemon pie.

Chanin Obermiller
Fairview, Oklahoma

SHAKER LEMON MERINGUE PIE

Sugar
4 1/2 tbsp. flour
Pinch of salt
3 eggs, separated
2 tbsp. margarine
1/4 c. lemon juice
2 tsp. lemon rind
1 baked 9-in. pie shell

Mix 1 cup sugar, flour and salt in double boiler. Stir in 1 1/4 cups water gradually. Add beaten egg yolks. Cook over hot water until thick, stirring constantly. Cook, covered, for 10 minutes longer. Add margarine, lemon juice and rind. Pour into pie shell. Beat egg whites until soft peaks form. Add 3 tablespoons sugar gradually,

beating until stiff. Spread over filling; seal to edge. Bake at 400 degrees until brown. Yield: 8 servings.

Zady E. Higginbotham
Adrian, Texas

TWO-CRUST LEMON PIE

1 1/4 c. sugar
2 tbsp. flour
1/8 tsp. salt
1/4 c. butter, softened
3 eggs
1 tsp. grated lemon rind
1 med. lemon, peeled, thinly sliced
1 recipe 2-crust pie pastry

Combine first 3 ingredients in bowl. Blend in butter. Reserve 1 teaspoon egg white. Beat remaining eggs together. Add to flour mixture with lemon rind and 1/2 cup water; mix well. Stir in lemon. Pour into pastry-lined 8-inch pie plate. Top with remaining pastry; seal edge and cut vents. Brush top with reserved egg white. Bake at 400 degrees for 30 to 35 minutes or until golden brown.

Vangie Welch
Bossier City, Louisiana

LIME CHIFFON PIE

5 eggs, separated
1 c. sugar
1/2 c. fresh lime juice
1 env. unflavored gelatin
2 or 3 drops of green food coloring (opt.)
Dash of salt
1 baked 9-in. pie shell

Beat egg yolks in double boiler; stir in 1/2 cup sugar and lime juice gradually. Cook over simmering water for 3 to 4 minutes or until thickened, stirring constantly. Soften gelatin in 1/4 cup cold water; stir into hot custard with food coloring. Cool. Beat egg whites with salt until soft peaks form. Add remaining 1/2 cup sugar gradually, beating until stiff. Fold in cooled custard. Pour into pie shell. Garnish with sliced limes and grated lime rind. Chill until serving time.

Celia Tutwiler
Jackson, Mississippi

FROZEN LIME PIE

FROZEN LIME PIE

  1 env. unflavored gelatin
  3/4 c. sugar
  1/8 tsp. salt
  1 c. milk
  1/3 c. fresh lime juice
  1 1/2 tsp. grated lime rind
  Several drops of green food coloring
  1 c. whipping cream, whipped
  1 egg white
  1 9-in. crumb pie shell

Combine gelatin, sugar and salt in saucepan; stir in milk. Heat until gelatin and sugar are dissolved. Chill until slightly thickened. Add lime juice, rind and food coloring. Fold in whipped cream. Beat egg white until soft peaks form. Fold into gelatin mixture. Spoon into pie shell. Freeze until firm. Garnish with additional whipped cream.

Photograph for this recipe above.

DIVINE LIME PIE

  4 eggs, separated
  1/4 tsp. cream of tartar
  1 1/2 c. sugar
  1/4 tsp. salt

  1/3 c. lime juice
  Green food coloring
  1 tbsp. grated lime rind
  2 c. whipping cream, whipped

Beat egg whites with cream of tartar until soft peaks form. Add 1 cup sugar gradually, beating until stiff. Spread in 10-inch pie plate, shaping 1-inch rim. Bake at 275 degrees for 20 minutes. Increase temperature to 300 degrees. Bake for 40 minutes longer or until light golden brown. Turn off oven; open oven door. Let stand in open oven to cool. Combine beaten egg yolks, salt, remaining 1/2 cup sugar and lime juice in double boiler; mix well. Cook over hot water for 10 minutes or until thick, stirring constantly. Cool. Tint pale green. Fold in lime rind and half the whipped cream. Spread over cooled shell; top with remaining whipped cream. Garnish with additional lime rind. Chill for 4 hours or longer.

Mady Barker
Vero Beach, Florida

SUMMERTIME LIME PIES

  1 lg. package lime gelatin
  1 c. sugar
  1 8-oz. package cream cheese, softened
  3 c. whipping cream, whipped
  1 tsp. vanilla extract
  4 9-in. graham cracker pie shells

Prepare gelatin using package directions. Chill until partially set. Mix sugar and cream cheese in bowl. Fold in whipped cream and vanilla. Add gelatin gradually, beating well. Pour into pie shells. Chill for 12 hours.

Karen Robinson
Sandy, Utah

KEY LIME PIE

  1 sm. can frozen limeade concentrate,
    thawed
  1 can sweetened condensed milk
  1 med. container whipped topping
  Dash of green food coloring
  1 8-in. graham cracker pie shell

Combine first 4 ingredients in bowl; mix well. Pour into pie shell. Chill until firm.

Linda Tuttle
Longwood, Florida

LIMEADE PIE

4 eggs, separated
1 c. sugar
1/4 c. cornstarch
1 6-oz. can limeade concentrate, thawed
1 tbsp. butter
Green food coloring
1 baked 9-in. pie shell

Beat egg yolks with 1/2 cup sugar, cornstarch and limeade in bowl. Stir into 1 cup boiling water in saucepan. Add butter. Cook until thick, stirring constantly. Stir in food coloring; cool. Beat remaining 1/2 cup sugar into beaten egg whites, beating until stiff. Fold half the beaten egg whites into cooked mixture. Spoon into pie shell. Top with remaining egg whites; seal to edge. Bake at 350 degrees until lightly browned.

Alma Eads
Audubon, Iowa

LIME COCONUT MERINGUE PIE

Sugar
1/3 c. cornstarch
1/2 tsp. salt
3 eggs, separated
1 tbsp. grated lime rind
Lime juice
3 tbsp. butter
Flaked coconut
1 baked 9-in. pie shell

Combine 1/2 cup sugar, cornstarch, salt and 1/4 cup cold water in double boiler; blend well. Stir in 1 1/4 cups hot water. Cook over boiling water until thick, stirring constantly. Beat egg yolks with 1/2 cup sugar in small bowl. Stir a small amount of hot mixture into beaten egg yolks; stir egg yolks into hot mixture. Cook for 2 to 3 minutes longer, stirring constantly; remove from heat. Stir in rind, 1/3 cup juice, butter and 1/2 cup coconut. Spoon into pie shell. Beat 1 tablespoon juice and 6 tablespoons sugar gradually into softly beaten egg whites; beat until stiff. Spoon lightly on filling; seal to edge. Sprinkle with coconut. Bake at 350 degrees for 10 minutes.

Geneva Haxton
Concordia, Kansas

LIME PARFAIT PIE

1 6-oz. package lime gelatin
1 tsp. grated lime rind
1/3 c. lime juice
1 qt. vanilla ice cream
1 baked 10-in. pie shell

Dissolve gelatin in 2 cups boiling water in bowl. Stir in lime rind and juice. Add ice cream by spoonfuls, stirring until melted. Chill until partially set. Spoon into pie shell. Chill until firm. Garnish with whipped cream and cherries.

Charlene McRae
Bainbridge, Georgia

MAPLE COCONUT PIE

1 c. flaked coconut
1 unbaked 9-in. pie shell
1/3 c. butter, softened
1/2 c. sugar
3 eggs, well beaten
1 c. maple syrup
1/2 tsp. vanilla extract

Sprinkle coconut over pie shell. Cream butter and sugar in bowl until fluffy. Add remaining ingredients; mix well. Pour into prepared pie shell. Bake at 425 degrees for 10 minutes. Reduce temperature to 350 degrees. Bake for 15 to 20 minutes longer or until set.

Monica Howard
Bay City, Michigan

MAPLE MACADAMIA PIE

1 c. chopped macadamia nuts
1 c. shredded coconut
1 unbaked pie shell
1 c. maple syrup
3 eggs, lightly beaten
1/4 c. sugar
1/4 tsp. salt
6 tbsp. melted butter

Layer nuts and coconut in pie shell. Chill for 15 minutes. Combine remaining ingredients in bowl; mix well. Pour into prepared shell. Bake at 400 degrees for 15 minutes. Reduce temperature to 350 degrees. Bake for 20 to 25 minutes or until set. Serve warm with whipped cream.

Hazel Newton
Danville, Pennsylvania

MAPLE CREAM PIE

1 1/2 c. milk, scalded
3/4 c. maple syrup
2 tbsp. cornstarch
1 egg
1/4 c. sugar
Dash of salt
1 baked 9-in. pie shell
1 c. heavy cream, whipped

Combine first 6 ingredients in double boiler. Cook until thick, stirring constantly. Pour into pie shell. Chill until serving time. Top with whipped cream.

Pam Thomas
Cazenovia, New York

VERMONT MAPLE CHIFFON PIE

1 tbsp. gelatin
1/2 c. milk
1/2 c. maple syrup
1/8 tsp. salt
2 eggs, separated
3/4 c. chopped nuts
1 tsp. vanilla extract
1 c. heavy cream, whipped
1 baked 9-in. pie shell

Soften gelatin in 1/4 cup cold water. Combine milk, maple syrup and salt in double boiler. Bring to a boil, stirring constantly. Pour hot syrup over beaten egg yolks, beating constantly. Cook in double boiler until thickened, stirring constantly. Add gelatin; stir until dissolved. Chill until partially set. Fold nuts and vanilla into whipped cream. Fold whipped cream and stiffly beaten egg whites into custard. Spoon into pie shell. Garnish with additional whipped cream. Chill until serving time.

Brook Stanford
Great Falls, Montana

CREAMY MINCEMEAT PIE

2 c. mincemeat
1 unbaked 9-in. Oatmeal Pie Shell (pg. 87)
1/3 c. packed brown sugar
2 tbsp. flour
3/4 c. whipping cream, whipped
1/2 c. broken pecans

Spoon mincemeat into pie shell. Combine brown sugar and flour with cream in bowl; blend well. Pour over mincemeat; sprinkle with pecans. Bake at 425 degrees for 15 minutes. Reduce temperature to 325 degrees. Bake for 15 minutes longer or until set.

May Hyden
Ashland, Kentucky

MINCEMEAT CHIFFON PIE

1 env. unflavored gelatin
1 1-lb. jar mincemeat
3 eggs, separated
2 tbsp. Brandy
1 tbsp. grated orange rind
1/2 c. sugar
1 c. whipping cream, whipped
1 baked 9-in. pie shell

Soften gelatin in 1/4 cup cold water. Combine mincemeat, egg yolks, Brandy and orange rind in saucepan. Cook until heated through, stirring constantly. Stir in gelatin. Refrigerate for 30 minutes. Beat egg whites and sugar until stiff peaks form; fold into mincemeat mixture. Fold half the whipped cream into mincemeat mixture. Pour into pie shell. Chill for 3 hours. Top with remaining whipped cream.

Cordelia Warren
Bainbridge, Georgia

MINCEMEAT-CHEESE PIE

4 3-oz. packages cream cheese, softened
1/2 c. sugar
2 eggs, beaten
Lemon rind
1 tbsp. lemon juice
1/2 tsp. vanilla extract
1 1/2 c. mincemeat
1 unbaked 9-in. pie shell

Beat cream cheese in mixer bowl until smooth. Add sugar, eggs, lemon rind, lemon juice and vanilla; beat well. Spread mincemeat in pie shell. Spoon cream cheese mixture evenly over mincemeat. Bake at 375 degrees for 35 minutes or until cheese layer is set. Chill until serving time.

Shawna Kent
Bangor, Maine

MINCEMEAT-SOUR CREAM PIE

2 c. prepared mincemeat
2 tbsp. Cognac
1 1/2 c. chopped toasted filberts
1 recipe 2-crust pie pastry
1 c. sour cream
1 egg
1/2 c. packed light brown sugar
1 tsp. vanilla extract

Combine mincemeat, Cognac and 1 cup filberts in bowl; mix well. Spoon into pastry-lined 9-inch pie plate. Combine sour cream, egg, brown sugar and vanilla in mixer bowl; beat until smooth. Fold in remaining 1/2 cup filberts. Spoon over mincemeat mixture. Cut remaining pastry into 1/2-inch wide strips. Twist slightly and arrange lattice-fashion over top. Seal to edge and flute crust. Bake at 400 degrees for 45 minutes.

Photograph for this recipe on page 2.

VENISON MINCEMEAT PIES

3 lb. ground cooked venison
6 lb. apples, sliced
1/2 lb. suet, chopped
5 lb. raisins
1/2 lb. citron, chopped
2 c. molasses
2 c. cider vinegar
2 lb. brown sugar
2 c. venison stock
1 tsp. each nutmeg, cinnamon, mace
1 tbsp. each salt, cloves
9 unbaked 9-in. pie shells

Combine first 9 ingredients in large pan; mix well. Stir in seasonings. Cook for 1 hour, stirring frequently. Spoon into pie shells. Bake at 425 degrees for 25 to 30 minutes or until crusts are browned.

Mrs. Sherman Gage
Waterbury, Vermont

MOLASSES CRUMB PIES

3 c. flour
1 c. sugar
1 c. margarine
1 tsp. soda
1 c. molasses
3 baked 8-in. pie shells

Combine flour and sugar in bowl. Cut in margarine until crumbly. Dissolve soda in 1 cup hot water. Mix with molasses until foamy. Reserve 1 cup flour mixture. Stir molasses mixture into remaining flour mixture. Pour into pie shells. Bake at 325 degrees for 8 minutes. Sprinkle with remaining flour mixture. Bake for 15 to 20 minutes longer or until crumbs are browned.

Ilona Tatum
Montrose, Colorado

SPICY MOLASSES PIE

3/4 c. flour
1/2 c. packed brown sugar
1/8 tsp. each nutmeg, ginger, cloves
1/2 tsp. cinnamon
1/4 tsp. salt
2 tbsp. shortening
1/2 tbsp. soda
1/2 c. molasses
1 egg yolk, beaten
1 unbaked 9-in. pie shell

Combine flour, brown sugar, spices and salt in bowl. Cut in shortening until crumbly. Dissolve soda in 3/4 cup boiling water; stir in molasses and egg yolk. Alternate layers of crumb mixture and molasses mixture in pie shell, ending with crumb mixture. Bake at 450 degrees until crust edge starts to brown. Reduce temperature to 350 degrees. Bake for 20 minutes longer.

Hilda Mountford
Morristown, New Jersey

OLD-FASHIONED MOLASSES PIE

1 1/4 c. molasses
2 tbsp. butter
4 eggs, beaten
2 tbsp. flour
2/3 c. sugar
1 unbaked pie shell

Bring molasses and butter to a boil in saucepan. Beat eggs until light and fluffy. Mix flour and sugar with eggs; add to molasses mixture. Pour into pie shell. Bake at 350 degrees for 30 minutes or until set.

Ann Potts
Allentown, Pennsylvania

CARIBBEAN MOCHA PIE

1/4 c. butter, softened
3/4 c. packed brown sugar
3 eggs
1 12-oz. package semisweet chocolate
    chips, melted
2 tsp. instant coffee powder
1 tsp. rum extract
1/4 c. flour
Pecans, chopped
1 unbaked 9-in. pie shell

Cream butter and sugar in bowl. Add eggs 1 at a time, beating well after each addition. Blend in next 3 ingredients. Stir in flour and 1 cup pecans. Pour into pie shell. Sprinkle with additional pecans. Bake at 375 degrees for 25 minutes; cool. Top with whipped cream.

Katherine A. Winchester
Winter Park, Florida

MOCHA CHIFFON PIE

1 env. unflavored gelatin
1/2 c. strong coffee
1 6-oz. package semisweet chocolate
    chips
4 eggs, separated
1/2 c. sugar
1/4 tsp. salt
1 tsp. vanilla extract
1 9-in. baked chocolate pie shell
Whipping cream, whipped
Peppermint candy, crushed

Soften gelatin in 1/4 cup cold water. Heat coffee and chocolate chips in saucepan until chocolate is melted, stirring constantly. Remove from heat; stir in gelatin until dissolved. Add beaten egg yolks, 1/4 cup sugar, salt and vanilla; mix well. Chill until slightly thickened. Beat egg whites until foamy. Add remaining 1/4 cup sugar gradually; beat until stiff. Fold egg whites into chocoalte mixture. Spoon into pie shell. Chill until firm. Top with whipped cream and crushed candy.

Mary Lou Kendrick
Garland, Alabama

FROZEN MOCHA PIE

1 6-oz. package semisweet chocolate
    chips
1 tbsp. instant coffee powder
Dash of salt
2 eggs, separated
1 7 1/2-oz. jar marshmallow creme
1 tsp. vanilla extract
1/8 tsp. almond extract
1 c. whipping cream, whipped
1 baked 9-in. pie shell

Combine first 3 ingredients with 1/4 cup water in double boiler. Cook over hot water until chocolate melts, stirring occasionally. Stir a small amount of hot mixture into beaten egg yolks; stir egg yolks into hot mixture. Cook for 3 minutes, stirring constantly; remove from heat. Blend in marshmallow creme and flavorings. Chill thoroughly. Fold in stiffly beaten egg whites and whipped cream. Spoon into pie shell. Freeze for 10 minutes or until firm.

Marvella Plapp
Leawood, Kansas

ORANGE CREAM MERINGUE PIE

1/2 c. sugar
1/4 c. cornstarch
1/4 tsp. salt
1 c. orange juice
1 c. milk, scalded
3 egg yolks, slightly beaten
1 tbsp. butter
1 tbsp. grated orange rind
1 baked 9-in. pie shell
1 recipe meringue

Mix first 3 ingredients in saucepan. Blend in orange juice and milk gradually. Cook over low heat until thick, stirring constantly. Stir a small amount of hot mixture into egg yolks; stir yolks into hot mixture. Cook over very low heat for 3 minutes longer, stirring constantly. Stir in butter and orange rind. Cool to lukewarm. Spoon into pie shell. Top with meringue; seal to edge. Bake at 400 degrees until lightly browned.

Mary Beth Spina
Sarasota, California

ORANGE AND APPLE PIE

1 recipe 2-crust pie pastry
1 c. honey
1 tbsp. lemon juice
5 oranges, thinly sliced, seeded
1/2 c. packed brown sugar
1/8 tsp. salt
1/4 tsp. cinnamon
1/8 tsp. ginger
4 apples, peeled, cored, sliced

Prepare and partially bake 9-inch pie shell using 2/3 of the pie pastry. Combine 3 cups water, honey and lemon juice in large saucepan. Bring to a boil; add orange slices. Simmer, covered, for 2 hours or until rind is tender. Drain. Combine brown sugar, salt and spices in bowl. Add apple slices; toss until coated. Alternate layers of apple and orange slices in pie shell until all ingredients are used. Top with remaining pastry; seal edge and cut vents. Bake at 350 degrees for 1 hour.

Lorna Thorne
Waycross, Georgia

ORANGE-COCONUT PIE

3 eggs, separated
1/4 tsp. salt
1/4 tsp. cream of tartar
1 3/4 c. sugar
1/4 c. cornstarch
2 c. orange juice
1 tsp. grated orange rind
1/2 pt. whipping cream, whipped
1/2 c. coconut flakes, toasted

Beat egg whites with 1/8 teaspoon salt and cream of tartar until stiff. Add 3/4 cup sugar gradually, beating until very stiff. Spread over bottom and up side of generously buttered 9-inch pie plate. Bake at 225 degrees for 1 hour. Cool completely. Combine remaining 1 cup sugar, 1/8 teaspoon salt and cornstarch in saucepan. Blend in orange juice, rind and beaten egg yolks. Bring to a boil over low heat, stirring constantly. Cook for 4 minutes, stirring constantly; cool. Pour into shell. Spread whipped cream over top. Sprinkle with coconut. Chill for several hours.

Dorthy Rickards
Marysville, California

ORANGE BLOSSOM PIE

2 c. orange sections
Sugar
1 3-oz. package cream cheese, softened
1 9-in. coconut-gingersnap pie shell (pg. 89)
2 1/2 tbsp. cornstarch
Orange juice

Sprinkle orange sections with 1/2 cup sugar in bowl. Let stand for 30 minutes. Spread cream cheese over bottom of pie shell. Drain sweetened orange sections, reserving liquid. Arrange over cream cheese. Blend cornstarch and 1/3 cup sugar in saucepan. Add enough orange juice to reserved liquid to measure 1 cup. Stir into sugar mixture. Cook until thick and clear, stirring constantly. Pour over oranges in pie shell. Garnish with additional orange sections. Chill until serving time.

Linda Grlep
Hartwell, Georgia

HOLIDAY ORANGE MERINGUE PIE

1/4 c. cornstarch
2 tbsp. flour
Sugar
1/4 tsp. salt
3 eggs, separated
1/3 c. strained orange juice
3 tbsp. butter
1/2 tsp. grated orange rind
1 baked 9-in. pie shell

Combine cornstarch, flour, 1 1/3 cups sugar and salt in double boiler; mix well. Add 1 1/2 cups boiling water gradually, stirring constantly. Cook until thick and clear, stirring constantly. Stir a small amount of hot mixture into beaten egg yolks; stir egg yolks into hot mixture. Cook for 2 minutes, stirring constantly; remove from heat. Stir in orange juice, butter and orange rind gradually; mix well. Cool. Pour into pie shell. Beat egg whites until soft peaks form; add 6 tablespoons sugar gradually, beating until stiff. Swirl over pie filling, sealing to edge. Broil until top is lightly browned.

Dorothy D. Perry
Winter Haven, Florida

FROZEN GOLDEN STRIPE PIE

1/2 c. frozen orange juice concentrate, thawed
4 c. sweetened whipped cream
1 qt. vanilla ice cream, softened
1 baked 9-in. pie shell
1 orange, thinly sliced

Fold concentrate into whipped cream. Alternate layers of whipped cream mixture and ice cream in pie shell until all ingredients are used, ending with whipped cream. Arrange orange slices over top. Freeze until firm.

Lenore Kellogg
Coeur d'Alene, Idaho

MANDARIN ORANGE PIE

4 oz. cream cheese, softened
1/3 c. lemon juice
1 can sweetened condensed milk
1   9-in. graham cracker pie shell
1   11-oz. can mandarin oranges
1/4 c. sugar
2 tbsp. cornstarch
1/2 tsp. lemon extract
1/4 c. slivered almonds

Blend cream cheese, lemon juice and condensed milk in bowl. Pour into pie shell. Drain mandarin oranges, reserving juice. Combine sugar and cornstarch in saucepan; stir in reserved juice. Cook over medium heat until thick and clear, stirring constantly. Cool. Add lemon extract and oranges. Spoon over cream cheese mixture. Sprinkle almonds over top. Chill for several hours.

Laura M. Fairbairn
Ione, Washington

BROWN SUGAR-OATMEAL PIE

2 tbsp. butter, softened
2/3 c. sugar
1 c. packed brown sugar
2/3 c. oats
2/3 c. coconut
1 tsp. vanilla extract
3 eggs, beaten
1 unbaked 9-in. pie shell

Cream butter and sugars in bowl. Mix in next 4 ingredients. Pour into pie shell. Bake at 350 degrees for 30 to 35 minutes.

Marcia Lynn
Lawrence, Massachusetts

OATMEAL-COCONUT PIE

1/2 c. sugar
1/4 tsp. salt
1/4 c. butter
3 eggs
1 c. corn syrup
1/2 c. oats
1/2 c. coconut
1 unbaked pie shell

Combine sugar, salt and butter in bowl; mix well. Add eggs 1 at a time, beating well after each addition. Blend in syrup. Stir in oats and coconut. Pour into pie shell. Bake at 350 degrees for 50 minutes or until filling is set.

Angela Black
Woonsocket, Rhode Island

PARADISE ISLAND PIE

2 egg whites, at room temperature
Dash of salt
1/4 tsp. cream of tartar
3/4 tsp. vanilla extract
1/2 c. sugar
3 tbsp. confectioners' sugar
1/2 pt. whipping cream
1 orange, chopped
2 ripe bananas, chopped
1 c. flaked coconut
1/2 c. pineapple tidbits, drained
1 tsp. grated orange rind

Combine egg whites, salt, cream of tartar and 1/4 teaspoon vanilla in mixer bowl; beat until soft peaks form. Add sugar, 1 teaspoon at a time, beating until stiff. Spread in 9-inch buttered pie pan, forming high edge. Bake at 275 degrees for 1 hour or until firm to touch. Cool. Combine confectioners' sugar, remaining vanilla and cream in bowl. Whip until stiff. Spread 1/3 of the mixture over pie shell. Mix orange and bananas with 1/2 cup coconut and pineapple in bowl. Place fruit mixture in pie shell. Spread remaining whipped cream mixture over fruit.

Sprinkle with remaining 1/2 cup coconut and orange rind. Chill for several hours or overnight.

Audrey Henderson
Jefferson, South Dakota

PARISIAN PEACH PIE

1 pt. French vanilla ice cream, softened
1 vanilla wafer pie shell
4 c. sliced peaches
1/2 c. pineapple juice
3 tbsp. syrup
3/4 c. finely chopped walnuts

Spoon ice cream into pie shell. Freeze until firm. Combine remaining ingredients in bowl. Chill in refrigerator. Spoon over ice cream to serve.

Troy Blair
Brookville, Pennsylvania

MARSHMALLOW PEACH PIE

16 marshmallows
1/2 c. milk
2 tbsp. sugar
3/4 c. whipped cream
1 1/2 c. chopped fresh peaches
1/2 tsp. vanilla extract
1   8-in. graham cracker pie shell
1/4 c. graham cracker crumbs
2 tbsp. melted butter

Melt marshmallows in milk in saucepan over medium heat. Cool. Stir 1 tablespoon sugar into whipped cream. Combine peaches and vanilla. Fold peaches and marshmallow mixture into whipped cream. Pour into pie shell. Mix crumbs with butter and 1 tablespoon sugar in bowl. Sprinkle over pie. Chill for 1 hour or longer.

LouAnn Restod
Columbia Heights, Minnesota

GINGER PEACHY PIE

2/3 c. sugar
2 tbsp. flour
2 tsp. ginger
1/8 tsp. salt
4 c. sliced peaches
1/2 c. chopped pecans

GINGER PEACHY PIE

1 recipe 2-crust pie pastry
1 tsp. lemon juice
1 tbsp. butter

Mix first 4 ingredients. Sprinkle over peaches and pecans in bowl; mix gently. Spoon into pastry-lined 9-inch pie plate. Sprinkle with lemon juice; dot with butter. Top with remaining pastry; seal edge and cut vents. Bake at 425 degrees for 30 minutes or until well browned.

Photograph for this recipe above.

FRENCH PEACH PIE

1 unbaked deep-dish pie shell
2 eggs
1 tbsp. lemon juice
1/3 c. sugar
4 c. frozen peaches, thawed
1 c. finely crushed vanilla wafers
1/2 c. chopped toasted almonds
1/4 c. butter, melted

Bake pie shell at 450 degrees for 5 minutes. Beat eggs and lemon juice together in bowl. Stir in sugar. Fold in peaches. Pour into pie shell. Combine remaining ingredients in bowl; mix well. Sprinkle over peach mixture. Bake at 375 degrees for 20 minutes. Top with cheese or ice cream.

Pamela Truhett
Woodland, Mississippi

DUTCH PEACH PIE

10 (or more) ripe peaches, peeled, sliced
1 unbaked 9-in. pie shell
1 egg, slightly beaten
1 c. sour cream
1/4 tsp. salt
3/4 c. sugar
5 tbsp. flour
1/2 tsp. each cinnamon, nutmeg
1/4 c. packed brown sugar
1/2 c. chopped pecans

Arrange peaches in pie shell. Combine egg, sour cream, salt, sugar, 2 tablespoons flour and spices in bowl; mix well. Pour over peaches. Bake at 350 degrees for 20 minutes. Mix remaining 3 tablespoons flour, brown sugar and pecans in small bowl. Sprinkle over pie. Bake for 15 to 20 minutes longer.

Christy Campbell
Sweetwater, Georgia

GLAZED PEACH PIE

4 c. sliced fresh peaches
3/4 c. sugar
1 pkg. orange gelatin
Dash of salt
4 tsp. lemon juice
1 baked 9-in. pie shell

Combine peaches and sugar in bowl. Let stand for 10 minutes. Dissolve gelatin and salt in 1 cup boiling water; add 1/2 cup cold water and lemon juice. Add peaches. Chill until slightly thickened. Turn into cold pie shell, arranging peaches as desired. Chill until firm. Garnish with whipped cream.

Marianne Prescott
Wichita, Kansas

PEACH CUSTARD PIE

1 lg. can sliced peaches
1 unbaked 8-in. pie shell
1/2 c. sugar
1/2 tsp. cinnamon
1/2 c. peach syrup
1 egg, slightly beaten
1 c. evaporated milk

Arrange peaches in pie shell. Sprinkle sugar and cinnamon over top. Bake at 375 degrees for 20 minutes. Combine peach syrup, egg and milk in bowl. Pour over peaches. Bake for 30 minutes longer.

Annette Page
Portland, Oregon

PEACH SURPRISE PIE

1 can sliced peaches, drained
1 baked 8-in. pie shell
1/4 c. orange juice
8 lg. marshmallows, chopped
1 sm. bottle of maraschino cherries,
*   quartered*
1/4 c. chopped pecans
1 c. whipped cream

Arrange peaches in pie shell. Pour orange juice over marshmallows in bowl. Let stand for several minutes. Fold cherries, pecans and marshmallow mixture into whipped cream. Spoon over peaches. Chill for several hours.

Anne Wilson
Little Rock, Arkansas

PEACH MERINGUE PIE

3 eggs, separated
Sugar
1 can evaporated milk
1 tsp. vanilla extract
1/2 tsp. almond flavoring
2 c. cooked dried peaches, mashed
1 unbaked 9-in. pie shell
Pinch of cream of tartar

Beat egg yolks. Add 3/4 cup sugar and milk; beat well. Add flavorings. Stir peaches into milk mixture. Pour into pie shell. Bake at 400 degrees for 15 minutes. Reduce temperature to 350 degrees. Bake until brown and firm. Beat egg whites until soft peaks form. Add 2 tablespoons sugar and cream of tartar. Beat until stiff. Spread on pie. Bake until lightly browned.

Sewanda Smith
Valdosta, Georgia

BAKED ALASKA PEACH PIE

1 1/2 c. sliced peaches
1/2 tsp. lemon juice
1/4 tsp. almond extract
1 qt. French vanilla ice cream, softened
1 graham cracker pie shell
6 egg whites, at room temperature
1/8 tsp. cream of tartar
6 tbsp. sugar
1 tsp. vanilla extract
1 drop each of red and yellow food coloring

Puree peaches with lemon juice in blender container. Add almond extract. Fold into ice cream. Pour into pie shell. Freeze until firm. Beat egg whites and cream of tartar until frothy. Add sugar 1 tablespoon at a time, beating until stiff. Add vanilla and food coloring. Pile meringue onto frozen pie. Bake in preheated 425-degree oven for 2 to 4 minutes or until lightly browned. Serve immediately.

Sherry Lodter
Roanoke, Virginia

PEACH PAN PIE

4 c. sliced canned peaches
2 c. sifted flour
3 tsp. baking powder
2 tsp. salt
Sugar
Grated rind of 1 orange
10 tbsp. shortening
1/2 tsp. cinnamon
2 tbsp. butter

Drain peaches, reserving syrup. Sift flour, baking powder, 1 teaspoon salt and 2 tablespoons sugar into bowl. Mix in orange rind. Cut in shortening until crumbly. Stir in 2/3 cup reserved peach syrup. Roll 1/8 inch thick on floured surface. Fit into 10-inch ovenproof skillet. Do not trim. Arrange peaches over dough. Combine 1/2 cup sugar, cinnamon and 1 teaspoon salt in bowl. Sprinkle over peaches. Dot with butter. Drizzle 1 tablespoon peach syrup over top. Fold excess dough toward center, leaving center open. Bake at 350 degrees for 35 to 40 minutes or until browned.

Mattie Mauldin
Harrisburg, Pennsylvania

MICROWAVE MELBA CHEESECAKE PIE

1/2 c. butter, melted
1 1/4 c. graham cracker crumbs
Sugar
1 16-oz. can sliced peaches, drained
1 8-oz. package cream cheese, softened
1/2 c. sour cream
1 egg
1/2 tsp. almond extract
1/3 c. raspberry jam

Combine butter, crumbs and 2 tablespoons sugar in bowl; mix well. Press over bottom and side of 9-inch pie plate. Microwave on High for 1 1/2 to 2 minutes or until hot. Arrange peaches over crust. Combine 1/3 cup sugar and remaining ingredients except jam in bowl; mix well. Pour over peaches. Microwave on High for 3 1/2 to 4 1/2 minutes or until edges are set, turning once. Spread jam over cooled pie. Chill in refrigerator.

Marilyn Jean Mancewicz
Grand Rapids, Michigan

PEACH MELBA PIE

3/4 c. cornflake crumbs
1/2 c. toasted blanched almonds, finely
  chopped
2 tbsp. packed light brown sugar
1/4 c. butter, melted
1 qt. vanilla ice cream, softened
1 16-oz. can peach slices, drained,
  chilled
Toasted whole blanched almonds
1/2 c. currant jelly
1 c. seedless red raspberry preserves

Combine first 4 ingredients in bowl; mix well. Press into bottom and side of 9-inch pie plate. Bake at 375 degrees for 8 minutes. Cool completely on wire rack. Spoon ice cream into crust, pressing until smooth. Freeze, covered, until firm. Soften in refrigerator for 30 minutes before serving. Arrange peach slices on pie. Garnish with almonds. Melt jelly in saucepan over low heat. Stir in raspberry preserves. Spoon over pie.

Lisa Davis
Raleigh, North Carolina

PEACHES AND CREAM PIE

1   3-oz. package lemon gelatin
1 c. peach syrup
1 pt. vanilla ice cream
1/8 tsp. almond extract
1   29-oz. can sliced peaches, drained
1 baked 9-in. pie shell

Dissolve gelatin in boiling peach syrup. Add 1/2 cup cold water and ice cream. Stir until melted. Stir in flavoring. Chill until partially set. Fold in peaches, reserving several for garnish. Pour into pie shell. Chill for 4 hours. Garnish with whipped cream and reserved peaches.

Nadine Spencer
Huntsville, Alabama

PEACHES AND PUDDING PIE

1 1/2 c. flour
1/2 tsp. salt
1/2 c. butter
1   16-oz. can peaches, drained, chopped
1/2 c. sugar
1/2 tsp. cinnamon
1/2 c. peach syrup
1 egg
1 c. evaporated milk

Combine flour and salt in bowl. Cut in butter until crumbly. Press into greased 9-inch pie plate. Arrange peaches over top. Mix sugar and cinnamon. Sprinkle over peaches. Bake at 375 degrees for 20 minutes. Combine peach syrup, egg and milk in mixer bowl. Beat for 1 minute. Pour over peaches. Bake for 30 minutes longer or until knife inserted in center comes out clean.

Susanne Gronemeyer
Prescott, Arizona

QUEEN ANNE PEACH PIE

Sliced peaches
1 unbaked 9-in. pie shell
2 eggs
1 c. sugar
1/4 c. melted butter
1 tbsp. flour
1/4 tsp. vanilla extract

Arrange peaches in 2 layers in pie shell, placing second layer over first in circular pattern. Combine remaining ingredients in bowl; mix well. Pour over peaches. Bake at 400 degrees for 20 minutes. Reduce temperature to 300 degrees. Bake for 40 minutes longer or until crust is brown and filling is set.

Jane West
Elizabeth, Pennsylvania

RANCH-STYLE PEACH PIE

3 egg whites
1 c. sugar
1/3 c. crushed soda crackers
1/2 c. finely chopped pecans
1/4 tsp. baking powder
1/4 tsp. vanilla extract
1   1-lb. can peach halves, drained,
*   thinly sliced*
1   8-oz. carton whipped topping

Beat egg whites in bowl until soft peaks form. Add sugar very gradually, beating until stiff. Fold in next 4 ingredients. Spread over bottom and side of greased 9-inch pie plate. Bake at 325 degrees for 30 minutes. Reserve several peach slices for garnish. Alternate layers of whipped topping and peaches on cooled crust, ending with topping. Chill until serving time. Garnish with reserved peach slices.

Judy Meek
Wichita, Kansas

THE BEST PEANUT BUTTER PIE

1 c. confectioners' sugar
1/2 c. peanut butter
1 baked 9-in. pie shell
2 c. milk
2 tbsp. butter
1/4 tsp. salt
1/4 c. cornstarch
2/3 c. sugar
3 egg yolks
1/4 tsp. vanilla extract
1 recipe meringue

Combine confectioners' sugar and peanut butter in bowl; mix until crumbly. Spread 3/4 of the mixture in pie shell. Scald milk with butter and salt in saucepan. Mix cornstarch and sugar in bowl. Blend in egg yolks. Stir into hot milk mixture gradually. Cook until thick, stirring constantly. Add vanilla. Pour into pie shell. Top with meringue; seal to edge. Sprinkle with remaining peanut butter mixture. Bake at 350 degrees for 15 minutes or until brown.

Helen Heath
Muncie, Indiana

PEANUT STREUSEL PIE

1/3 c. peanut butter
3/4 c. sifted confectioners' sugar
1 baked 9-in. pie shell
1/3 c. flour
1 c. sugar
1/8 tsp. salt
2 c. milk, scalded
3 eggs, separated
2 tbsp. butter
1/2 tsp. vanilla extract
1/4 tsp. cream of tartar
1 tbsp. cornstarch

Blend peanut butter with confectioners' sugar in bowl until crumbly. Sprinkle 2/3 of the mixture over pie shell. Mix flour, 1/2 cup sugar and salt in double boiler. Blend in milk gradually. Cook over boiling water until thick, stirring constantly. Stir a small amount of hot mixture into beaten egg yolks; stir egg yolks into hot mixture. Cook for several minutes longer. Stir in butter and vanilla. Pour into pie shell. Beat cream of tartar into stiffly beaten egg whites. Add 1/2 cup sugar mixed with cornstarch gradually, beating constantly until very stiff and glossy. Spoon onto pie. Sprinkle with remaining peanut butter mixture. Bake at 350 degrees for 15 to 20 minutes. Chill until serving time.

Barbara Blum
Northfield, Vermont

PEANUT BUTTER BONBON PIE

3 1/4 c. flour
1 tsp. salt

2/3 c. shortening
1/2 c. peanut butter
6 egg yolks
1 c. sugar
1 tsp. vanilla extract
2 c. milk, scalded
1/2 c. coconut
2 Mars candy bars, chopped
1/2 c. roasted peanuts, finely ground

Combine 2 cups flour and salt in bowl. Cut in shortening and peanut butter until crumbly. Add 1 1/4 cups cold water; mix well. Roll on floured surface. Fit into 9-inch pie plate. Bake at 450 degrees for 10 minutes or until browned. Combine egg yolks and sugar in saucepan; beat well. Add remaining 1 1/4 cups flour, vanilla and milk; mix well. Heat to boiling point, stirring constantly. Stir in coconut. Cool for 10 minutes. Spoon into pie shell. Sprinkle candy over warm pie. Top with peanuts.

Carol Waters
Rye, New York

PEAR FLUFF PIE

3 fresh Bartlett pears, peeled, halved
Lemon juice
1   3-oz. package peach gelatin
1/4 tsp. salt
1/2 pt. whipping cream
3 tbsp. sugar
2 tbsp. Sherry (opt.)
1 baked 9-in. pie shell

Chop 2 1/2 pears. Chill remaining pear half, wrapped, in refrigerator. Combine chopped pears with 2 tablespoons lemon juice and 1 cup water in saucepan. Simmer for 5 minutes. Remove pears with slotted spoon. Add enough water to hot liquid to measure 1 cup. Stir in gelatin and salt until gelatin dissolves. Chill until thick. Whip cream with sugar in bowl until stiff. Reserve 1/2 cup for topping. Fold remaining whipped cream, Sherry and cooked pears into gelatin. Pour into pie shell. Chill until firm. Slice remaining pear. Coat with lemon juice. Arrange with reserved whipped cream on top of pie.

Velma Smith
Jonesboro, Arkansas

CRISPY PINK PIE

CRISPY PINK PIE

    1   30-oz. can pear halves, drained
    1   unbaked 9-in. pie shell
    1   20-oz. can strawberry pie filling
    1   tbsp. lemon juice
    3/4 c. flour
    1/2 c. sugar
    1   tsp. cinnamon
    1/3 c. butter

Cut pear halves in half lengthwise; arrange in pie shell. Mix pie filling and lemon juice; spoon over pears. Combine flour, sugar and cinnamon in bowl; cut in butter until crumbly. Sprinkle over top. Bake at 425 degrees for 30 minutes or until lightly browned.

Photograph for this recipe above.

FRESH PEAR PIE

    4   lg. fresh pears, peeled, thinly sliced
    3   tbsp. frozen orange juice concentrate
    1   unbaked 9-in. pie shell
    1/2 c. sugar
    Dash of salt
    3/4 c. flour
    1/2 c. butter
    1   tsp. cinnamon

Mix pears with orange juice concentrate in bowl. Arrange in pie shell. Blend sugar, salt, flour, butter and cinnamon in bowl. Sprinkle over pears. Bake at 400 degrees for 40 minutes or until pears are tender.

Mary O'Connor
Butte, Montana

CREAMY PEAR PIE

3/4 c. sugar
1 tbsp. cornstarch
1 tsp. nutmeg
Dash of salt
1/2 c. cream
2 tbsp. lemon juice
1 29-oz. can pears
1 recipe 2-crust pie pastry

Mix sugar, cornstarch, nutmeg and salt in bowl. Combine cream and lemon juice. Stir into dry ingredients; mix well. Drain and slice pears. Add to cream mixture. Pour into pastry-lined pie plate. Cover with lattice crust. Bake at 425 degrees for 30 to 35 minutes.

Bobbie Jackson
Garden City, New Jersey

STREUSEL PEAR PIE

1/2 c. sugar
1 tsp. cinnamon
2 tbsp. lemon juice
1 1/2 tbsp. Minute tapioca
6 c. sliced Bartlett pears
1 unbaked 9-in. pie shell
1/2 c. packed brown sugar
1 c. flour
1/2 c. butter

Combine sugar, cinnamon, lemon juice, tapioca and pears in bowl. Let stand for 15 minutes. Pour into pie shell. Combine brown sugar and flour in bowl. Cut in butter until crumbly. Pat evenly over pears. Bake at 375 degrees for 45 minutes or until browned.

Christy Clarke
Pelham, Tennessee

PEAR PIE WITH HOT CINNAMON SAUCE

4 or 5 fresh pears, sliced
3/4 c. sugar
2 tbsp. flour
1/2 tsp. cinnamon
1 recipe 2-crust pie pastry
1 tbsp. butter
Hot Cinnamon Sauce

Combine first 4 ingredients in bowl; toss to coat. Arrange in pastry-lined 9-inch pie pan. Dot with butter. Top with remaining pastry; seal edge. Cut slits in top. Bake at 400 degrees for 45 minutes. Serve warm with Hot Cinnamon Sauce.

Hot Cinnamon Sauce

1/2 c. sugar
1 tbsp. cinnamon
1 tbsp. cornstarch
2 tbsp. butter
1 tsp. vanilla extract

Combine first 3 ingredients in saucepan. Stir in 1 cup hot water. Cook until thick and clear, stirring constantly. Add butter and vanilla. Cook for 2 to 3 minutes longer.

Cynthia L. Ward
Stillwater, Oklahoma

CALIFORNIA PEAR PIE

6 lg. Bartlett pears
1/2 c. dried apricots
1/4 c. butter, softened
1/3 c. sugar
1/4 tsp. salt
2 tbsp. lemon juice
8 whole cloves
1/4 c. packed brown sugar
1 1/2 tbsp. cornstarch
1 baked 9-in. pie shell

Peel, halve and core pears; stuff with apricots. Spread butter over bottom of 10-inch skillet; sprinkle with half the sugar. Place pears in skillet; sprinkle with remaining sugar, salt, lemon juice and cloves. Add 1 cup water; cover. Bring to a boil. Simmer for 20 minutes or until just tender. Remove pears with slotted spoon; drain well, reserving liquid. Discard cloves. Add enough water to reserved liquid to measure 1 1/4 cups. Blend brown sugar and cornstarch; add to pear liquid. Cook over medium heat until mixture comes to a boil, stirring constantly. Spoon half the sauce into pie shell. Arrange pears in shell. Spoon remaining sauce over pears. Cool before cutting.

Bonnie Franklin
Oakland, California

DEEP-DISH PEAR PIE

2 lb. pears, peeled, halved
1 tbsp. lemon juice
3 tbsp. flour
1 c. sugar
Dash of salt
1/2 tsp. cinnamon
1/2 tsp. nutmeg
1 tbsp. butter
Cheddar cheese pie pastry

Arrange pears in deep pie plate. Sprinkle with lemon juice. Mix flour, sugar, salt, cinnamon and nutmeg together; sprinkle over pears. Dot with butter. Place pastry over pears; crimp to edge of pie plate. Slash in several places. Bake at 350 degrees for 30 to 40 minutes. Serve with cream.

Sylvia Sutton
Miami, Florida

QUICK PEAR PIE

2 c. chopped pears
Sugar
1 egg, beaten
1 c. cream
Flour
1 tsp. vanilla extract
1/8 tsp. salt
1 unbaked pie shell
1/4 c. butter

Combine pears, 1/2 cup sugar, egg, cream, 1 tablespoon flour, vanilla and salt in bowl; mix well. Pour into pie shell. Bake at 350 degrees for 15 minutes. Combine 2/3 cup flour, 1/3 cup sugar and butter in bowl; mix until crumbly. Sprinkle over pie. Bake for 30 minutes longer or until browned.

Provi Whorley
Oakland, California

BUTTERSCOTCH PECAN PIE

3 eggs, beaten
1 c. light corn syrup
1/8 tsp. vanilla extract
1 c. packed brown sugar
2 tbsp. butter, melted

1 c. pecan halves
1 unbaked 9-in. pie shell

Combine first 5 ingredients in bowl in order listed; mix well. Stir in pecans. Pour into pie shell. Bake at 400 degrees for 15 minutes. Reduce temperature to 350 degrees. Bake for 30 to 35 minutes longer or until set. Cool on wire rack. Garnish with whipped cream rosettes.

Umbergine McClurkan
Albany, New York

GEORGIA PECAN PIE

2 eggs, beaten
1 c. light corn syrup
1/8 tsp. salt
1 tsp. vanilla extract
1/2 c. packed brown sugar
1/2 c. sugar
2 tbsp. melted butter
1 c. broken pecans
1 unbaked 9-in. pie shell

Combine first 8 ingredients in bowl; mix well. Pour into pie shell. Bake at 400 degrees for 15 minutes. Reduce temperature to 350 degrees. Bake for 30 minutes longer.

Scott Church
Bainbridge, Georgia

CHOCOLATE AND BOURBON PECAN PIE

1 c. sugar
1/4 c. butter, melted
3 eggs, slightly beaten
3/4 c. light corn syrup
1/4 tsp. salt
2 tsp. Bourbon
1 tsp. vanilla extract
1/2 c. chopped pecans
1/2 c. chocolate chips
1 unbaked 9-in. pie shell

Cream sugar and butter in bowl. Add eggs, corn syrup, salt, Bourbon and vanilla; mix well. Spread pecans and chocolate chips in pie shell. Pour filling into shell. Bake at 375 degrees for 40 to 50 minutes or until set.

Mary Margaret Gibson
Crestfield, Nevada

QUICK CHERRY-PECAN PIES

1 sm. can evaporated milk
1 can sweetened condensed milk
1 c. chopped pecans
1 can sour pie cherries, drained
Pinch of salt
Juice of 3 lemons
2 graham cracker pie shells

Blend evaporated milk and condensed milk in bowl. Stir in pecans, cherries and salt. Fold in lemon juice. Pour into pie shells. Chill until set.

Linda Owens
Mt. Vernon, Texas

MICROWAVE SOUTHERN PECAN PIE

1 unbaked 9-in. pie shell
Dried beans
4 tbsp. butter
1 tbsp. flour
3 eggs, beaten
1 c. dark corn syrup
2/3 c. sugar
1/2 tsp. vanilla extract
1 c. pecan halves

Line pie shell with plastic wrap. Fill to 1-inch depth with dried beans. Microwave on Medium for 3 minutes, turning once. Remove wrap and beans. Microwave for 3 minutes longer. Microwave butter in glass mixing bowl on High for 1 minute. Blend in flour. Cool slightly. Stir in eggs, corn syrup and sugar. Microwave, uncovered, on Medium for 10 minutes or until slightly thick, stirring occasionally. Add vanilla; mix well. Pour into prepared pie shell. Arrange pecans over top. Microwave on Medium-Low for 8 minutes or until just set, turning once.

Theresa Benson
Ryan, Oklahoma

MOLASSES-PECAN PIE

3 eggs, beaten
3/4 c. dark corn syrup
1/4 c. molasses

1/2 c. sugar
Pinch of salt
1 tsp. vanilla extract
1 1/4 c. broken pecans
1 unbaked 10-in. pie shell

Combine eggs, corn syrup and molasses in bowl; mix well. Stir in next 4 ingredients; mix well. Pour into pie shell. Bake at 400 degrees for 15 minutes.

Zella Rhinehardt
St. Louis, Missouri

MYSTERY PECAN PIE

1 8-oz. package cream cheese, softened
Sugar
4 eggs
2 tsp. vanilla extract
1/4 tsp. salt
1 unbaked 9-in. pie shell
1 1/4 c. chopped pecans
1 c. light corn syrup

Beat cream cheese, 1/3 cup sugar, 1 egg, 1 teaspoon vanilla and salt in bowl until creamy. Spread in pie shell. Sprinkle pecans over top. Combine 3 beaten eggs, 1/4 cup sugar, corn syrup and 1 teaspoon vanilla in bowl. Beat until well blended. Pour over pecans. Bake at 375 degrees for 35 to 40 minutes or until center is firm.

Shama Greene
Chicago, Illinois

ORANGE-PECAN PIE

1 c. light corn syrup
1/4 c. butter
1/4 c. sugar
1 c. chopped pecans
1 tbsp. orange juice
1 tbsp. grated orange rind
3 eggs, well beaten
1/2 tsp. salt
1 unbaked 9-in. pie shell

Combine first 8 ingredients in medium bowl; mix well. Pour into pie shell. Bake at 350 degrees for 45 minutes.

Gladys Brown
Jenks, Oklahoma

PECAN CUSTARD PIE

3 eggs, well beaten
1 c. sugar
1/4 c. butter
1 c. milk
3 tbsp. flour
1 tsp. vanilla extract
1/4 c. maple syrup
1/4 c. quick-cooking oats
1/4 c. pecans
1/4 c. coconut
1 unbaked pie shell

Combine first 7 ingredients in bowl; mix well. Stir in oats, pecans and coconut. Pour into pie shell. Bake at 350 degrees until set.

Barbie Lamle
Okeene, Oklahoma

PRALINE BUTTER PECAN PIE

2 tbsp. light brown sugar
2 tbsp. butter
1/3 c. chopped pecans
1 partially baked 9-in. pie shell
1 1/2 c. cold milk
1 c. vanilla ice cream, softened
1 lg. package butter pecan instant
  pudding mix

Combine brown sugar, butter and pecans in saucepan. Heat until butter is melted. Pour into pie shell. Bake at 450 degrees for 5 minutes. Cool. Blend milk and ice cream in mixer bowl. Add pudding mix. Beat at low speed for 1 minute or until blended. Pour into pie shell. Chill for 3 hours or until set. Garnish with whipped topping and pecan halves.

Photograph for this recipe on Cover.

FRENCH MINT PIE

1/2 c. butter, softened
1 c. confectioners' sugar
3 egg yolks
2 sq. unsweetened chocolate, melted
1/4 tsp. peppermint flavoring
1 graham cracker pie shell
Whipped cream

Cream butter and sugar in bowl. Add egg yolks 1 at a time, beating well after each addition. Add chocolate to creamed mixture. Stir in flavoring. Pour into pie shell. Top with whipped cream. Chill in refrigerator.

Aggie Elliott
Frasier, Ohio

CANDY CANE PIE

1 env. unflavored gelatin
2 sq. unsweetened chocolate
3/4 c. sugar
1 c. milk
2 eggs, separated
1/4 tsp. salt
1 c. whipping cream, whipped
1 c. crushed peppermint candy canes
1   9-in. graham cracker pie shell

Soften gelatin in 1/2 cup cold water. Combine chocolate, 1/2 cup sugar and milk in double boiler. Heat over boiling water until chocolate melts. Beat until smooth. Stir beaten egg yolks into chocolate mixture gradually. Cook for 3 minutes, stirring constantly. Add gelatin; stir until dissolved. Chill until thickened. Add salt to egg whites. Beat until stiff. Beat in 1/4 cup sugar gradually. Fold egg whites and half the whipped cream into chocolate mixture. Fold in 1/2 cup candy. Spoon filling into pie shell. Chill until firm. Garnish pie with remaining whipped cream and candy.

Margaret Koonce
Tyler, Texas

FLUFFY PEPPERMINT PIE

1 env. unflavored gelatin
3 egg whites, stiffly beaten
1 c. whipping cream, whipped
1/2 tsp. vanilla extract
1 c. crushed peppermint candy
1/2 tsp. mint flavoring
1 unbaked 9-in. graham cracker pie shell

Soften gelatin in 1/4 cup cold water. Fold into egg whites. Fold in next 4 ingredients. Pour into pie shell. Refrigerate until serving time.

Annie Dobson
Mebone, North Carolina

MINT-CHIP PIE

1 c. whipping cream
1 tbsp. sugar
1 c. milk
1/2 tsp. peppermint extract
3 drops of green food coloring
1 pkg. vanilla instant pudding mix
1/2 c. semisweet chocolate chips
1 baked 8-in. pie shell

Whip cream and sugar until soft peaks form; set aside. Combine milk, peppermint extract and food coloring in bowl. Add pudding mix. Beat with rotary beater for 1 minute or until blended. Fold whipped cream mixture and chocolate chips into pudding. Pour into pie shell. Chill until firm.

Jayne Brofry
Boise, Idaho

RICH PEPPERMINT PIE

4 c. miniature marshmallows
1/2 c. milk
1 c. heavy cream, whipped
1/2 c. crushed peppermint candy
1 9-in. chocolate cookie pie shell

Combine 3 cups marshmallows and milk in double boiler. Heat until marshmallows are melted, stirring constantly. Chill until slightly thickened. Fold in whipped cream, remaining marshmallows and candy. Pour into pie shell. Chill until firm.

Muriel Freedman
Omaha, Nebraska

COMPANY'S COMING PIE

3 egg whites
1/2 tsp. cream of tartar
1 1/4 c. sugar
1 tsp. vanilla extract
18 saltine crackers, crushed
1 c. pecans
1/2 pt. whipping cream, whipped
1 sm. can crushed pineapple
1 c. coconut

Beat egg whites and cream of tartar until soft peaks form. Add 1 cup sugar gradually, beating until stiff. Fold in vanilla, crackers and pecans. Spread in buttered 9-inch pie plate. Bake at 325 degrees for 30 to 35 minutes. Beat 1/4 cup sugar into whipped cream in bowl. Fold in pineapple with juice. Spread over cooled crust. Sprinkle with coconut. Chill for several hours.

Mae Bailey
Denver, Colorado

PINEAPPLE-OATMEAL PIE

2/3 c. sugar
1 c. packed brown sugar
3 eggs, beaten
2 tbsp. melted butter
1 tsp. vanilla extract
2/3 c. oats
2/3 c. coconut
1 c. raisins
1 8 1/4-oz. can crushed pineapple
1 unbaked 9-in. pie shell

Add sugars to eggs; beat well. Blend in butter and vanilla. Stir next 4 ingredients into egg mixture. Pour into pie shell. Bake at 350 degrees for 50 minutes. Cool on wire rack.

Diane E. Mills
Pavilion, New York

DREAMY PINEAPPLE PIE

1 c. sugar
1/2 c. flour
1 sm. can crushed pineapple
Salt to taste
3 eggs, separated
1 baked 9-in. pie shell
1 carton whipped topping

Combine first 4 ingredients and egg yolks in double boiler; mix well. Stir in 1 1/2 cups boiling water gradually. Cook until thickened, stirring constantly. Cool. Fold in stiffly beaten egg whites. Pour into pie shell. Spread whipped topping over filling.

Erla Click
Bluefield, West Virginia

PINEAPPLE LIME PIE

PINEAPPLE LIME PIE

1   8 3/4-oz. can crushed pineapple
1 env. unflavored gelatin
3/4 c. sugar
1/3 c. fresh lime juice
Several drops of green food coloring
1 1/2 c. crushed coconut bar cookies
1/4 c. butter, melted
1 c. evaporated milk, partially frozen

Drain pineapple reserving juice. Mix gelatin, sugar, lime juice and food coloring with reserved juice in saucepan. Cook over low heat until sugar and gelatin dissolve, stirring constantly. Chill until thickened. Mix cookie crumbs with melted butter. Press over bottom and side of 9-inch pie plate. Chill until firm. Whip evaporated milk until stiff. Fold in gelatin mixture and pineapple. Spoon into prepared pie plate. Chill for 2 hours or until firm.

Photograph for this recipe above.

RICH PINEAPPLE PIE

2 c. sugar
1/2 c. margarine, softened
6 eggs
1 tbsp. flour
1 c. flaked coconut

1 c. crushed pineapple, drained
1 unbaked 9-in. pie shell

Cream sugar and margarine in bowl. Add eggs 1 at a time, beating well after each addition. Add flour. Mix in coconut and pineapple gradually. Pour into pie shell. Bake at 350 degrees for 35 minutes.

Jackie Jeffries
Reno, Nevada

CREAMY PINEAPPLE PIE

1 sm. package vanilla instant pudding mix
1 8-oz. can crushed pineapple
2 c. sour cream
1 tbsp. sugar
1 baked 9-in. pie shell

Combine pudding mix, undrained pineapple, sour cream and sugar in bowl. Beat slowly with rotary beater until smooth. Pour into pie shell. Chill until firm.

Patricia Swahn
San Antonio, Texas

PINEAPPLE-COCONUT PIES

3 eggs, beaten
1 c. sugar
1 stick butter, softened
2 tbsp. flour
1 lg. can coconut
1 lg. can pineapple, drained
2 unbaked deep-dish pie shells

Combine first 6 ingredients in order listed in bowl; mix well. Pour into pie shells. Bake at 300 degrees for 1 hour.

Marilyn Rulse
Macclenny, Oklahoma

PINEAPPLE-SOUR CREAM PIE

1 c. sugar
1/4 c. flour
1/2 tsp. salt
1 20-oz. can crushed pineapple, drained
1 c. sour cream

2 eggs, separated
1 baked 9-in. pie shell
1/2 tsp. vanilla extract
1/4 tsp. cream of tartar

Combine 3/4 cup sugar, flour and salt in saucepan. Stir in next 2 ingredients. Bring to a boil, stirring constantly. Cook for 2 minutes longer. Stir a small amount of hot mixture into beaten egg yolks; stir egg yolks into hot mixture. Cook for 2 minutes, stirring constantly. Cool to room temperature. Spoon into pie shell. Beat egg whites, vanilla and cream of tartar in bowl until soft peaks form. Add remaining 1/4 cup sugar gradually, beating until stiff. Spread over pie, sealing to edge. Bake at 350 degrees for 12 to 15 minutes or until browned.

Stacey Barnett
Cleveland, Ohio

PISTACHIO-ALMOND PIE

Flour
5 eggs, separated
2 c. milk
1/2 c. blanched almonds
1/2 c. blanched pistachio nuts
1/3 c. sugar
Dash of salt
1 c. (about) butter, softened

Mix 1 3/4 cups flour with egg whites in bowl until smooth. Shape into ball. Let stand, covered, for 2 hours. Blend 6 tablespoons flour with several teaspoons milk in small bowl then mix with remaining milk in saucepan. Cook over low heat for 10 minutes or until thick, stirring constantly; cool. Grind almonds and pistachio nuts in food processor to make fine paste. Stir in sugar and salt. Mix egg yolks 1 at a time into cooled milk mixture; stir in nut paste. Divide dough into 12 portions. Layer 6 very thinly rolled portions alternately with 1 heaping tablespoon butter in generously buttered 9-inch pie plate. Spread with nut mixture. Repeat layers with remaining 6 portions dough and butter, ending with butter. Bake at 400 degrees for 35 minutes or until golden brown. Serve warm or cold.

Pauline Donnelly
Shalimar, Florida

PISTACHIO CREAM PIES

1 env. unflavored gelatin
1 c. sugar
6 egg yolks, beaten
2 c. whipping cream, whipped
Pistachio nuts, chopped
1/2 c. dark rum
2 baked 9-in. pie shells

Soften gelatin in 1/2 cup cold water in saucepan. Heat over low heat until gelatin dissolves. Cool. Beat sugar into egg yolks until light. Stir in gelatin mixture. Fold in whipped cream and pistachio nuts. Blend in rum. Chill until partially set. Spoon into pie shells. Chill until firm. Garnish with shaved bittersweet chocolate and pistachio nuts.

Evelyn Bell
Hereford, Texas

FRESH DAMSON PLUM PIE

1 qt. fresh damson plums, quartered
4 c. sugar
1 unbaked 9-in. pie shell

Combine plums and sugar in saucepan. Cook until plums are tender, stirring frequently. Spoon into pie shell. Bake at 450 degrees until crust is golden. Garnish with whipped cream.

Diedre Somer
Kanab, Utah

PLUM PRESERVE PIE

1/2 c. butter, softened
1 1/2 c. sugar
5 eggs, separated
1 tbsp. flour
1/8 tsp. salt
1 c. damson plum preserves
1 unbaked 9-in. pie shell

Cream butter with 3/4 cup sugar. Beat egg yolks with remaining 3/4 cup sugar. Beat egg yolk mixture into creamed mixture. Add flour and salt; mix well. Blend in preserves. Fold in stiffly beaten egg whites. Spoon into pie shell. Bake at 350 degrees until set. Garnish with whipped cream.

Tracy Regis
Forest City, Arkansas

PRUNE PIE

1/2 c. packed brown sugar
2 tbsp. cornstarch
1 c. prune juice
2 tbsp. butter
1 c. chopped cooked prunes
1 orange, peeled, chopped
1 baked 9-in. pie shell
1 recipe meringue

Mix brown sugar, cornstarch and juice in saucepan. Cook over low heat until thickened. Add butter, prunes and orange. Cook over low heat for 5 minutes. Pour into pie shell. Top with meringue. Bake at 350 degrees for 20 minutes.

Mari Austin
Eureka, California

BROWN SUGAR-PUMPKIN CHIFFON PIE

3/4 c. packed brown sugar
1 1/2 c. mashed cooked pumpkin
1/2 c. milk
1/2 tsp. salt
1 tsp. cinnamon
1/2 tsp. nutmeg
3 eggs, separated
1 env. unflavored gelatin
1/4 c. sugar
1 baked 9-in. pie shell

Combine first 6 ingredients and beaten egg yolks in double boiler. Cook until thick, stirring constantly. Soften gelatin in 1/4 cup cold water. Add to hot mixture; stir to dissolve. Beat egg whites until soft peaks form. Add sugar gradually, beating until stiff. Fold into pumpkin mixture. Pour into pie shell. Chill until firm.

Ophelia Sansing
Senatoba, Mississippi

CRUNCHY PUMPKIN PIE

1 1/2 c. flour
1/2 c. oil
1 1/2 tsp. salt
1   16-oz. can pumpkin
2 eggs, beaten
2 tsp. pumpkin pie spice
1 can sweetened condensed milk

1 box vanilla instant pudding mix
2 tbsp. butter
1/2 c. packed brown sugar
1/3 c. chopped pecans

Place flour in 9-inch pie plate. Bring oil, 1 teaspoon salt and 1/4 cup water to a boil in saucepan. Pour over flour; mix well. Pat over bottom and side of pie plate. Combine next 5 ingredients and 1/2 teaspoon salt in large bowl; mix well. Pour over crust. Bake at 425 degrees for 15 minutes. Reduce temperature to 350 degrees. Bake for 45 minutes longer. Combine butter, brown sugar and pecans in bowl. Spread over pie. Broil for 1 minute.

Judy Sandlin
Del City, Oklahoma

CHEESY PUMPKIN PIES

1   8-oz. package cream cheese, softened
1/2 tsp. vanilla extract
1 egg
3/4 c. sugar
2 unbaked 9-in. pie shells
1 1/4 c. mashed cooked pumpkin
1 tsp. cinnamon
1/4 tsp. each ginger, nutmeg
1/8 tsp. salt
1 c. light cream
2 tbsp. maple syrup
1/2 c. chopped pecans

Combine first 3 ingredients and 1/4 cup sugar in bowl; mix well. Pour into pie shells. Mix pumpkin, spices, salt, remaining 1/2 cup sugar and cream in bowl. Pour over cream cheese mixture. Bake at 350 degrees for 65 to 70 minutes. Brush with maple syrup; sprinkle with pecans.

Frieda Sparks
Salem, Oregon

GRANDMA'S PUMPKIN PIES

2 1/2 tsp. pumpkin pie spice
1 1/2 c. packed brown sugar
1/2 tsp. salt
2 tbsp. flour
1 c. sugar
3 1/2 c. mashed cooked pumpkin
3 eggs, beaten
1 stick butter, melted

1/2 can evaporated milk
2 unbaked 9-in. pie shells

Combine first 5 ingredients in bowl; mix well. Add pumpkin, eggs, butter and evaporated milk; mix well. Pour into pie shells. Bake at 350 degrees for 1 hour or until set. Serve with whipped cream.

Janet Jones
Lexington, Kentucky

GOLDEN NUGGET PIE

1 env. unflavored gelatin
1 c. sugar
2 eggs, separated
1 tsp. pumpkin pie spice
1/2 tsp. salt
3/4 c. evaporated milk
1 1-lb. can pumpkin
1 1/2 tsp. grated orange rind
1 baked 9-in. pecan pie shell

Soften gelatin in 1/4 cup water in 2-quart saucepan. Stir in 1/2 cup sugar, egg yolks and seasonings until smooth. Add evaporated milk. Cook over low heat until thick, stirring constantly. Remove from heat. Stir in pumpkin and orange rind. Chill until thick. Beat egg whites until soft peaks form. Add 1/2 cup sugar gradually, beating until stiff. Fold in pumpkin mixture. Spoon into pie shell. Garnish with chopped pecans. Chill for 2 to 3 hours or until firm.

Cee Jay Wilkinson
Arlington, Virginia

ORANGE-PUMPKIN PIE

3 tbsp. margarine, melted
1 1/2 c. mashed cooked pumpkin
2/3 c. sugar
1/4 tsp. cinnamon
1/2 tsp. allspice
1/2 c. evaporated skim milk
1/2 c. Egg Beaters
1 3-oz. package orange gelatin
1 baked 9-in. pie shell
1/4 c. finely chopped pecans

Combine margarine, pumpkin, sugar, cinnamon, allspice, skim milk and Egg Beaters in saucepan; mix well. Bring to a full boil over low heat, stirring constantly. Chill until cool. Dissolve gelatin in 1 cup boiling water. Chill until slightly thickened. Place bowl in large bowl of ice and water. Beat until thick and fluffy. Fold in chilled pumpkin mixture. Spoon into pie shell. Sprinkle with pecans. Chill until firm.

Octavia Lyons
Daytona Beach, Florida

PUMPKIN CHEESECAKE PIE

1 8-oz. package cream cheese, softened
1/2 c. sugar
1 egg
1 tsp. vanilla extract
1 unbaked 9-in. pie shell
2 c. pumpkin
1 can sweetened condensed milk
1 egg
1/2 tsp. each salt, nutmeg, cinnamon,
   ginger

Combine first 4 ingredients in bowl; mix well. Spread in pie shell. Mix pumpkin, condensed milk, egg, salt and spices in bowl. Pour over cream cheese layer. Bake at 375 degrees for 50 to 55 minutes or until knife inserted in center comes out clean. Chill overnight.

Betty Cummings
Keene, New Hampshire

PARTY PUMPKIN CHIFFON PIE

1 env. unflavored gelatin
2/3 c. sugar
1/2 tsp. salt
1/2 tsp. ginger
3 eggs, separated
1/2 c. Triple Sec
1 1/4 c. canned pumpkin
1/2 c. whipping cream, whipped
1 9-in. gingersnap crumb pie shell

Combine gelatin, 1/3 cup sugar, salt and ginger in double boiler. Stir in 1/4 cup water. Beat in egg yolks 1 at a time. Stir in Triple Sec. Cook until slightly thickened, stirring constantly. Remove from heat. Stir in pumpkin. Cool. Beat remaining 1/3 cup sugar into stiffly beaten egg whites gradually. Beat until very stiff. Fold in pumpkin mixture and whipped cream. Spoon into pie shell. Chill until firm.

Priscilla Peters
Fresno, California

PUMPKIN SURPRISE PIE

FROZEN PUMPKIN PIE

1 pt. vanilla ice cream, softened
1 baked 9-in. pie shell
1 c. canned pumpkin
1/2 tsp. each nutmeg, allspice,
*   cinnamon, salt*
1/4 tsp. ginger
1 1/4 c. sugar
1/2 pt. whipping cream, whipped

Mold ice cream over bottom and up side of pie shell. Combine remaining ingredients except whipped cream in large bowl; mix well. Fold in whipped cream. Pour into ice cream-filled crust. Freeze for 24 hours or longer. Remove from freezer 20 minutes before serving.

Barbara E. Smoot
Selma, Indiana

PUMPKIN SURPRISE PIE

1/2 lb. marshmallows
1 1/4 c. cooked pumpkin
1/2 tsp. salt
1/2 tsp. cinnamon
1/4 tsp. ginger
1/2 c. nonfat dry milk powder
1 baked 9-in. pie shell
12 pecan halves

Combine marshmallows, pumpkin and seasonings in double boiler. Cook over boiling water until marshmallows are melted, stirring occasionally; cool. Dissolve milk powder in 1/2 cup water. Whip until stiff. Fold in cooled pumpkin mixture. Spoon into pie shell. Chill until serving time. Top with pecan halves.

Photograph for this recipe above.

LAYERED WALNUT-PUMPKIN PIE

1 env. unflavored gelatin
1 1-lb. can pumpkin
3/4 c. sugar
1/2 c. milk
3 eggs, separated
1 tsp. pumpkin pie spice
1/2 tsp. salt
1/4 tsp. vanilla extract
3/4 c. walnuts, finely chopped
1 c. whipping cream
1 baked 9-in. pie shell

Soften gelatin in 1/4 cup cold water in 2-quart saucepan. Stir in pumpkin, 1/2 cup sugar, milk, lightly beaten egg yolks, spice and salt. Heat to boiling point, stirring constantly. Cook over very low heat for 5 minutes, stirring constantly. Blend in vanilla. Chill until slightly thickened. Beat 2 tablespoons sugar into stiffly beaten egg whites. Fold into pumpkin mixture with walnuts. Whip cream with 2 tablespoons sugar until stiff. Layer half the pumpkin mixture and 3/4 of the whipped cream in pie shell. Spoon remaining pumpkin mixture on top. Decorate with remaining whipped cream and walnut halves. Chill for 4 hours or longer.

Corina Wendland
Corpus Christi, Texas

SPICY PUMPKIN CHIFFON PIE

3 eggs, separated
1 c. sugar
1 1/4 c. canned pumpkin
1/2 c. milk
1/2 tsp. each salt, ginger, cinnamon,
*   nutmeg*
1 env. unflavored gelatin
1 baked 9-in. pie shell

Combine beaten egg yolks and 1/2 cup sugar in double boiler; beat until thick. Add pumpkin, milk, salt and spices; mix well. Cook until thick, stirring constantly. Soften gelatin in 1/4 cup cold water. Stir into pumpkin mixture until dissolved. Beat egg whites with remaining 1/2 cup sugar until stiff. Fold into pumpkin mixture. Pour into pie shell. Chill until firm.

Dixie Austin
Wells, Nevada

QUINCE PIE

2 lb. unripe quinces, peeled, quartered
4 c. sugar
2 or 3 whole cloves
1 cinnamon stick
12 egg yolks
1 unbaked 10-in. pie shell

Combine quinces with 2 1/2 cups sugar, cloves and cinnamon in saucepan. Cook for 30 minutes or until thick, stirring frequently. Cool. Beat egg yolks with remaining 1 1/2 cups sugar in saucepan. Cook over very low heat until slightly thickened, stirring constantly. Cool to room temperature, stirring occasionally. Spoon quince mixture into pie shell, removing cloves and cinnamon. Spread egg mixture over top. Bake at 350 degrees for 30 minutes or until topping is puffed and golden. Serve warm.

Faith Redfield
Aberdeen, South Dakota

SOUR CREAM-RAISIN PIE

2 tbsp. cornstarch
1 c. sugar
1/4 tsp. salt
1 tsp. cinnamon
1/2 tsp. nutmeg
1/4 tsp. cloves
2 eggs, separated
1 c. sour cream
1 c. raisins
1 1/2 tsp. lemon juice
1/2 c. chopped walnuts
1 baked 9-in. pie shell
1/4 tsp. cream of tartar

Combine cornstarch, 3/4 cup sugar, salt and spices in double boiler. Add beaten egg yolks; mix well. Add sour cream, raisins and lemon juice. Cook over hot water until smooth and thick, stirring constantly. Cool slightly. Stir in walnuts. Pour into pie shell. Beat egg whites until frothy; add cream of tartar. Beat until stiff peaks form. Add remaining 1/4 cup sugar gradually, beating until glossy. Spread meringue over filling. Bake at 300 degrees for 15 minutes or until lightly browned.

Florence Potter
Middleburg, Pennsylvania

HARVEST MOON RAISIN PIE

DOG-TICK PIE

1 1/2 c. sugar
4 tbsp. flour
1 egg, well beaten
3 tbsp. lemon juice
2 tsp. grated lemon rind
1/8 tsp. salt
1 c. raisins
1 recipe 2-crust pie pastry

Blend first 3 ingredients in double boiler. Add next 4 ingredients with 2 cups water; mix well. Cook for 15 minutes or until thick, stirring occasionally. Cool for 5 to 10 minutes. Pour into pastry-lined 9-inch pie plate. Top with lattice crust. Bake at 450 degrees for 10 minutes. Reduce temperature to 350 degrees. Bake for 20 minutes longer or until lightly browned.

Phyllis A. Stratton
Muskogee, Oklahoma

HARVEST MOON RAISIN PIE

1 1/3 c. raisins
3 egg yolks
1 c. sugar
2 tbsp. flour
2 tbsp. vinegar
2 tbsp. butter
1 baked 9-in. pie shell
1 recipe meringue

Simmer raisins in 2 cups water in saucepan for 5 minutes. Beat egg yolks, sugar, flour and vinegar in bowl until light and creamy. Stir into raisins. Cook for 5 minutes or until thickened, stirring constantly. Remove from heat; blend in butter. Cool slightly. Pour into pie shell. Spread meringue over top. Bake at 425 degrees for 4 to 5 minutes or until meringue is delicately browned. Cool on rack.

Photograph for this recipe above.

JAPANESE RAISIN PIES

2 sticks butter, softened
2 c. sugar
4 eggs, beaten
2 tbsp. vinegar
1 c. raisins
1 c. nuts
1 c. coconut
2 unbaked 9-in. pie shells

Beat butter, sugar and eggs in bowl until smooth. Stir in vinegar, raisins, nuts and coconut. Pour into pie shells. Bake at 275 degrees for 40 minutes or until set.

Wilma Davis
Watertown, Tennessee

CREAMY RAISIN PIE

1 c. seedless raisins
1 c. sugar
1 tbsp. flour
1 c. half and half
1/3 stick margarine, melted
1 tsp. vanilla extract
1 unbaked 9-in. pie shell

Boil raisins in 1/2 cup water in saucepan until raisins puff. Mix sugar and flour in bowl. Add raisins, half and half, margarine and vanilla; mix well. Pour into pie shell. Bake at 350 degrees until crust is golden brown and pie tests done.

Cammie Alley
Missoula, Montana

COTTAGE CHEESE-RAISIN PIE

1 1/2 c. small curd cottage cheese
2 tbsp. milk
2 tbsp. sour cream
2 eggs, beaten
1 tbsp. flour
1/2 c. sugar
Pinch of salt
1 tsp. grated lemon rind
3 tbsp. lemon juice
1/4 tsp. vanilla extract
1/2 c. raisins, plumped
1 partially baked 9-in. pie shell
Grated nutmeg

Combine cottage cheese, milk, sour cream and eggs in bowl; mix well. Add flour, sugar and salt; mix well. Stir in lemon rind, juice, vanilla and raisins. Pour into pie shell. Sprinkle nutmeg on top. Bake at 350 degrees for 30 minutes or until knife inserted in center comes out clean.

Eleonor Showalter
Lancaster, Pennsylvania

SAUCY RAISIN-ICE CREAM PIE

1 egg white
1/4 tsp. salt
1/4 c. sugar
1 1/2 c. chopped walnuts
1 pt. coffee ice cream
1 pt. vanilla ice cream
3 tbsp. butter
1 c. packed light brown sugar
1/2 c. heavy cream
1 tsp. vanilla extract
1/2 c. golden raisins

Beat egg white and salt until soft peaks form. Add sugar gradually, beating until stiff. Fold in walnuts. Spread in buttered pie plate. Bake at 400 degrees for 10 to 12 minutes or until lightly browned; cool. Alternate scoops of coffee and vanilla ice cream over top. Combine butter and brown sugar in saucepan. Cook until blended. Remove from heat; stir in cream gradually. Heat for 1 minute. Stir in vanilla and raisins. Spoon warm sauce over ice cream.

Laurena Dale
Clarksburg, West Virginia

BLACK RASPBERRY CUSTARD PIE

2 eggs, beaten
1 c. sugar
2 tbsp. flour
1 c. evaporated milk
2 c. black raspberries
1 unbaked 8-in. pie shell

Beat eggs, sugar, flour and milk in bowl. Spread raspberries in pie shell. Pour sugar mixture over top. Bake at 350 degrees for 40 minutes or until set.

Wylma Colehour
Mt. Carroll, Illinois

BLACK RASPBERRY CREAM PIE

2/3 c. sugar
1/4 c. sifted flour
1/4 tsp. salt
1 3/4 c. milk
3 egg yolks, slightly beaten
2 tbsp. butter
1 tbsp. lemon juice
2 c. drained black raspberries
1 baked 8-in. pie shell
1 recipe meringue

Mix first 3 ingredients in saucepan. Heat 1 1/2 cups milk until scalded. Stir 1/4 cup cold milk into sugar mixture. Add scalded milk, mixing well. Cook over low heat until thick, stirring constantly. Stir a small amount of hot mixture into egg yolks; stir egg yolks into hot mixture. Cook over very low heat for 3 minutes, stirring constantly. Add butter and lemon juice; blend well. Cool to lukewarm. Arrange raspberries in pie shell. Spoon filling over berries. Top with meringue. Bake at 400 degrees until light brown.

Althea Veedt
Burns, Oregon

RASPBERRY-ALMOND PIE

1 c. flour
Sugar
1/2 tsp. grated lemon rind
1/3 c. plus 1 tbsp. butter
1 egg yolk, slightly beaten
1/2 c. raspberry jam
4 egg whites
1/2 tsp. almond extract
3/4 c. blanched almonds, ground

Mix flour, 2 teaspoons sugar and lemon rind in bowl. Cut in butter until crumbly. Blend in egg yolk. Roll on lightly floured board. Fit into 9-inch pie pan. Trim edges and flute; prick shell with fork. Spread jam on bottom of shell. Chill in refrigerator. Beat egg whites until foamy; add flavoring. Add 1/2 cup sugar gradually, beating until stiff. Fold in almonds. Spoon over jam. Bake at 375 degrees for 30 to 40 minutes. Serve cool.

Carol Kendrick
Montgomery, Alabama

FRESH RASPBERRY PIE

1 c. sugar
3 tbsp. cornstarch
1/2 c. crushed raspberries
1 qt. fresh raspberries
1 baked 8-in. pie shell

Combine 1 cup water, sugar and cornstarch in saucepan. Cook until thick, stirring constantly. Stir in crushed raspberries. Arrange whole raspberries in pie shell. Pour sugar mixture over berries. Bake at 350 degrees for 30 minutes or until crust is lightly browned. Serve with ice cream or whipped cream.

Ella Post
Red Oak, Iowa

RASPBERRY-BUTTERMILK PIE

1 c. buttermilk
1 c. raspberries
1 c. sugar
3 tbsp. flour
3 egg yolks
1 tbsp. butter
1 baked 9-in. pie shell
1 recipe meringue

Combine buttermilk, raspberries, sugar, flour, egg yolks and butter in double boiler over hot water. Cook until thick, stirring constantly. Spoon into pie shell. Spread meringue over filling, sealing to edge. Bake at 350 degrees for 15 minutes.

Sharon Spencer
Goshen, Indiana

RASPBERRY MERINGUE PIE

1 1/4 c. sifted flour
1/4 tsp. soda
1/4 tsp. salt
1/2 c. margarine, softened
Sugar
1 tsp. vanilla extract
2 eggs, separated
2 tbsp. cornstarch
1   10-oz. package frozen raspberries,
*   thawed*
1/2 c. chopped walnuts

Sift flour, soda and salt together. Cream margarine with 1/3 cup sugar in bowl. Add vanilla. Add beaten egg yolks to creamed mixture, mixing well. Add sifted ingredients; mix well. Press into 10-inch pie plate. Mix 1/4 cup sugar and cornstarch in saucepan; add raspberries. Cook over low heat until thickened, stirring constantly. Spoon into prepared pie plate. Top with walnuts. Beat egg whites until soft peaks form; add 2 tablespoons sugar gradually, beating until stiff. Spread over walnuts. Bake at 350 degrees for 30 minutes.

Cheri Platt
Corning, New York

RASPBERRY VELVET PIE

1   10-oz. package frozen raspberries,
    thawed
1 pkg. raspberry gelatin
1/4 lb. marshmallows
1 c. heavy cream, whipped
1   9-in. crumb pie shell

Drain raspberries, reserving juice. Add enough water to reserved juice to measure 1 cup. Dissolve gelatin in 1 cup boiling water. Stir in marshmallows until partially melted. Mix in raspberry juice. Chill until partially set. Beat until fluffy. Fold in raspberries and whipped cream. Spoon into pie shell. Chill until firm. Garnish with additional whipped cream.

Laurel Prentiss
Norwich, Connecticut

RASPBERRY CHIFFON PIE

1   10-oz. package frozen red
    raspberries, thawed
1   3-oz. package raspberry gelatin
2 tbsp. lemon juice
1 sm. carton whipped topping
2 egg whites
Dash of salt
1/4 c. sugar
1 baked 9-in. pie shell

Drain raspberries, reserving juice. Add enough water to reserved juice to measure 2/3 cup. Dissolve gelatin in 3/4 cup boiling water. Stir in

lemon juice and raspberry juice. Chill until partially set. Beat until fluffy. Fold in raspberries and half the whipped topping. Beat egg whites with salt and sugar until stiff. Fold into raspberry mixture. Spoon into pie shell. Chill for several hours. Top with remaining whipped topping.

Renee Lipchitz
Traverse City, Michigan

PINEAPPLE-RHUBARB PIE

3 c. chopped rhubarb
1 c. drained pineapple tidbits
1 recipe 2-crust pie pastry
3 tbsp. flour
1 c. sugar
1 egg, beaten
1 tbsp. butter

Spread rhubarb and pineapple in pastry-lined 9-inch pie plate. Sprinkle with mixture of flour and sugar. Beat egg with 1 tablespoon water. Pour over rhubarb mixture. Dot with butter. Top with lattice crust. Bake at 450 degrees for 10 minutes. Reduce temperature to 375 degrees. Bake for 40 minutes longer.

Millie Wray
Scottsbluff, Nebraska

RHUBARB CREAM PIE

1 c. sugar
2 tbsp. flour
1 tbsp. butter
3 egg yolks
2 c. chopped rhubarb
1 unbaked 8-in. pie shell
1 recipe meringue

Combine sugar and flour in bowl. Cut in butter until crumbly. Add egg yolks; mix well. Stir in rhubarb. Pour into pie shell. Bake at 450 degrees for 10 minutes. Reduce temperature to 350 degrees. Bake for 30 minutes longer. Top with meringue, sealing to edge. Bake at 450 degrees until meringue browns.

Phyllis Garriott
Brentwood, Tennessee

RHUBARB BUTTERSCOTCH PIE

4 c. chopped fresh rhubarb
1 unbaked 9-in. pie shell
1/2 c. packed brown sugar
3 tbsp. flour
1/8 tsp. salt
2 eggs, well beaten
3 tbsp. heavy cream

Spread rhubarb in pie shell. Combine remaining ingredients in bowl; mix well. Spread over rhubarb. Bake at 450 degrees for 10 minutes. Reduce temperature to 350 degrees. Bake for 20 to 25 minutes longer.

Louise Knox
Muncie, Indiana

RHUBARB CUSTARD PIE

3 c. chopped rhubarb
1 unbaked 9-in. pie shell
1 1/2 c. sugar
3 tbsp. flour
1/2 tsp. nutmeg
1/4 tsp. salt
1 tbsp. butter, softened
2 eggs, beaten

Spread rhubarb in pie shell. Combine remaining ingredients in bowl; beat well. Pour over rhubarb. Bake at 450 degrees for 10 minutes. Reduce temperature to 350 degrees. Bake for 30 minutes or until knife inserted halfway to center comes out clean.

Elnora Snyder
Loudonville, Ohio

SURPRISE RHUBARB PIE

2 eggs
1 1/2 c. sugar
1/4 c. flour
3/4 tsp. baking powder
Salt to taste
3 c. chopped rhubarb
1 baked 9-in. crumb pie shell

Beat eggs in bowl until fluffy. Sift in next 4 ingredients; mix well. Stir in rhubarb. Spoon into pie shell. Bake at 350 degrees for 35 minutes.

Leola Wolfgram
Rochester, Minnesota

EASY RHUBARB PIE

2 c. chopped rhubarb
1 unbaked 8-in. pie shell
1 c. sugar
1/3 c. flour
1/2 pt. whipping cream, whipped

Spread rhubarb in pie shell. Fold sugar and flour into whipped cream. Pour over rhubarb. Bake at 425 degrees for 10 minutes. Reduce temperature to 350 degrees. Bake for 30 to 40 minutes longer.

Lucy Calhoun
Kelso, Washington

RAISIN-RHUBARB MERINGUE PIE

4 c. chopped rhubarb
1 c. raisins
1 1/2 c. sugar
1/3 c. cornstarch
1/4 tsp. salt
2 egg yolks, slightly beaten
1 unbaked 9-in. pie shell
1 recipe meringue

Combine rhubarb, raisins and 3/4 cup water in saucepan. Cook until rhubarb is tender-crisp. Drain, reserving liquid. Blend reserved liquid with sugar, cornstarch and salt in saucepan. Cook until thick, stirring constantly. Stir a small amount of hot mixture into egg yolks; stir egg yolks into hot mixture. Add rhubarb and raisins; mix well. Pour into pie shell. Bake at 450 degrees for 10 minutes. Reduce temperature to 350 degrees. Bake for 25 to 30 minutes longer. Top with meringue; seal to edge. Bake until meringue is lightly browned.

Liz Madison
Fredonia, Kansas

RHUBARB MERINGUE PIES

4 eggs, separated
3 c. sugar
1/2 c. milk
3 tbsp. flour
4 c. chopped rhubarb
2 baked Rich Sweet Pie Shells (pg. 93)
1/4 tsp. (heaping) cream of tartar
Dash of salt
1 tsp. vanilla extract

Combine beaten egg yolks, 2 cups sugar, milk and flour in bowl; mix well. Fold in rhubarb. Pour into pie shells. Bake at 350 degrees for 40 minutes. Beat egg whites and cream of tartar until stiff peaks form. Add salt and vanilla. Beat in remaining 1 cup sugar gradually. Spread over rhubarb mixture, sealing to edge. Bake at 350 degrees for 20 minutes.

Harriet Jones
Waterloo, Iowa

SHOOFLY PIE

1 1/2 c. flour
1/2 c. sugar
1/8 tsp. salt
1/2 tsp. cinnamon
1/4 tsp. each ginger, nutmeg
1/4 c. margarine, softened
1 unbaked 8-in. pie shell
1/2 c. molasses
1/2 tsp. soda

Combine first 6 ingredients in bowl; mix well. Cut in margarine until crumbly. Spread 1 1/3 cups mixture in pie shell. Combine molasses, soda and 3/4 cup boiling water in bowl; mix well. Pour over crumb mixture. Sprinkle remaining crumbs over top. Bake at 375 degrees for 30 to 40 minutes or until lightly browned.

Vivian C. Pike
Claremont, North Carolina

SOUR CREAM PIE

1/2 c. butter, softened
1 1/2 c. sugar
2 eggs, separated
1/2 c. sour cream
1 tbsp. flour
1 tsp. cinnamon
1 unbaked 9-in. pie shell

Cream butter and sugar in bowl. Add beaten egg yolks, 1/4 cup sour cream, flour and cinnamon; mix well. Fold in remaining sour cream and stiffly beaten egg whites. Pour into pie shell. Bake at 350 degrees for 30 minutes.

Florence Redfern
Tarkio, Missouri

FRESH STRAWBERRY PIE

1 c. sugar
3 tbsp. cornstarch
2 tbsp. light corn syrup
Pinch of salt
2 tsp. strawberry gelatin
Red food coloring
3 c. fresh strawberries
1 baked 8-in. pie shell

Combine first 4 ingredients and 1 cup water in saucepan. Cook over low heat until thick and clear, stirring constantly. Cool slightly. Stir in gelatin and food coloring until gelatin dissolves. Arrange strawberries in pie shell. Pour glaze over top. Garnish with whipped cream and additional strawberries.

Marilyn Frisbee
Cabool, Missouri

STRAWBERRY CHEESECAKE PIE

1 8-oz. package cream cheese, softened
1 carton whipped topping
1/2 carton sour cream
3/4 c. sugar
1/4 c. lemon juice
1 9-in. graham cracker pie shell
Strawberries

Beat cream cheese in bowl until fluffy. Add next 4 ingredients 1 at a time, beating well after each addition. Pour into pie shell. Chill until firm. Top with strawberries.

Enid Woodward
Pampa, Texas

STRAWBERRY LATTICE PIE

2 1/2 c. sliced strawberries
1/2 c. sugar
1/4 tsp. salt
2 1/2 tbsp. Minute tapioca
1 tsp. grated lemon rind
1 recipe 2-crust pie pastry

Combine first 5 ingredients in bowl; mix well. Spoon into pastry-lined 9-inch pie plate. Top with lattice crust. Bake at 450 degrees for 10 minutes. Reduce temperature to 350 degrees. Bake for 30 minutes longer.

Sheryl Burt
San Antonio, Texas

STRAWBERRY-COFFEE PIE

STRAWBERRY-COFFEE PIE

1 env. unflavored gelatin
4 tsp. instant coffee powder
1 8-oz. package cream cheese, softened
1/2 c. sugar
Dash of salt
1 1/2 tsp. vanilla extract
1 c. whipping cream, whipped
1 pt. fresh California strawberries
1 baked 9-in. pie shell

Sprinkle gelatin and coffee powder over 1 cup water in small saucepan. Heat until gelatin dissolves, stirring constantly. Beat cream cheese, sugar, salt and vanilla in bowl until fluffy. Stir in gelatin mixture gradually. Chill until thickened. Fold in whipped cream. Reserve 8 to 10 whole strawberries for garnish; cut remaining berries in half. Pour half the coffee filling into pie shell; top with halved strawberries. Cover with remaining coffee filling. Chill for 3 hours or until firm. Arrange remaining strawberries on top.

Photograph for this recipe above.

STRAWBERRY ANGEL PIE

1 c. whipping cream
1 to 2 tbsp. confectioners' sugar
1 pt. fresh strawberries, sliced
1 meringue pie shell (pg. 90)

Beat cream and confectioners' sugar in bowl until stiff. Fold in strawberries. Spread in pie shell. Chill until serving time.

Lacey Gibson
Haines City, Florida

STRAWBERRY CHIFFON PIE

1 env. unflavored gelatin
1 1/2 c. strawberry preserves
3 tbsp. lemon juice
1/8 tsp. salt
3 egg whites, stiffly beaten
1 c. heavy cream, whipped
1 baked 9-in. pie shell

Soften gelatin in 2 tablespoons cold water in small saucepan. Cook over very low heat until dissolved, stirring frequently; remove from heat. Stir in preserves, lemon juice and salt. Chill for 30 minutes or until partially set. Fold strawberry mixture into stiffly beaten egg whites. Fold strawberry mixture into whipped cream. Chill for 15 minutes or until partially set. Spoon into pie shell. Chill until firm. Garnish with additional whipped cream and mint sprigs.

Cecilia Neal
Medina, Ohio

STRAWBERRY-ICE CREAM PIE

1 3-oz. package strawberry gelatin
1 pt. vanilla ice cream
1 pt. strawberries
1 9-in. graham cracker pie shell
2 c. whipped cream

Dissolve gelatin in 1 cup boiling water in bowl. Stir in ice cream until melted. Add strawberries. Pour into pie shell. Chill until firm. Top with whipped cream.

Carol Swanson
Butler, Pennsylvania

CREAMY STRAWBERRY PIE

1/2 lb. marshmallows
1/4 c. milk
1 qt. strawberries, halved
1/2 pt. whipping cream, whipped
1 9-in. graham cracker pie shell

Melt marshmallows in milk in double boiler. Cool. Fold strawberries and marshmallow mixture into whipped cream. Pour into pie shell. Chill for 4 hours or longer.

Nora Broome
Steamboat Springs, Colorado

STRAWBERRY-WHIPPED CREAM PIE

2 pt. strawberries
2 c. sweetened whipped cream
1 baked 9-in. Poppy Seed Pie Shell (pg. 96)
2 tbsp. (or more) honey
Toasted slivered almonds

Fold 2 cups sliced strawberries into whipped cream. Spread evenly in cooled pie shell.

Arrange 2 cups halved strawberries, cut side down, over top. Drizzle with honey and sprinkle with almonds.

Madge Shamokin
New Castle, Pennsylvania

CREAMY SWEET POTATO PIES

3 1/2 c. mashed cooked sweet potatoes
1/2 c. butter, softened
2 c. sugar
4 eggs
1/2 tsp. each nutmeg, salt
1 lg. can evaporated milk
2 tsp. lemon extract
2 unbaked 9-in. pie shells

Combine first 3 ingredients in bowl; mix well. Add eggs 1 at a time, beating well after each addition. Stir in nutmeg, salt, milk and flavoring. Pour into pie shells. Bake at 425 degrees for 20 minutes. Reduce temperature to 325 degrees. Bake for 30 to 45 minutes or until pies test done.

Lucille H. Wiggins
Portsmouth, Virginia

OLD-FASHIONED SWEET POTATO PIE

2 eggs, beaten
2 tsp. allspice
1 1/2 sticks butter, melted
2 3-oz. packages cream cheese, softened
2 c. sugar
1 tsp. vanilla extract
1 tbsp. cornstarch
1 1/2 c. mashed sweet potato
1 c. flaked coconut
1 unbaked 9-in. pie shell

Combine eggs, allspice, butter, cream cheese, sugar and vanilla in bowl; mix well. Mix cornstarch with 1/4 cup hot water until smooth. Add to egg mixture with sweet potato and coconut; mix well. Pour into pie shell. Bake at 425 degrees for 10 minutes. Reduce temperature to 325 degrees. Bake for 35 to 45 minutes longer.

Rena Black
Rockford, Illinois

SAVORY SWEET POTATO PIE

EASY SWEET POTATO PIES

1 1/2 c. mashed cooked sweet
   potatoes
1/2 c. packed brown sugar
1/2 c. sugar
2 tbsp. margarine, melted
1/4 tsp. salt
1/2 tsp. nutmeg
1 tsp. vanilla extract
1/2 tsp. cinnamon
1 1/2 c. milk
3 egg yolks
2 unbaked pie shells

Combine first 10 ingredients in bowl; mix well.
Pour into pie shells. Bake at 350 degrees until
set.

Louise H. Capps
Elizabeth City, North Carolina

SAVORY SWEET POTATO PIE

2 c. mashed cooked sweet potatoes
1/2 c. butter, softened
3 eggs, separated
3 tbsp. sugar
1/4 c. chopped onion
1/4 c. chopped parsley
1 tsp. salt
1/4 tsp. tarragon
1 tbsp. fresh lemon juice
1/2 c. milk
1 unbaked 9-in. pie shell

Beat sweet potatoes with butter until smooth.
Beat in egg yolks, sugar, onion, parsley, salt,
tarragon, lemon juice and milk. Fold in stiffly
beaten egg whites. Spoon into pie shell. Bake at
350 degrees for 50 minutes.

Photograph for this recipe above.

SPICY SWEET POTATO PIE

2 tbsp. butter, melted
1 1/2 c. mashed cooked sweet potatoes
1/2 c. packed brown sugar
1 tsp. cinnamon
1/2 tsp. ginger
1/4 tsp. mace
1/4 tsp. salt
2 eggs, beaten
1 1/2 c. milk, scalded
1 unbaked 10-in. pie shell

Blend butter into sweet potatoes. Mix brown sugar with spices, salt and eggs in bowl. Add to sweet potato mixture gradually; beat well. Beat in milk. Pour into pie shell. Bake at 450 degrees for 10 minutes. Reduce temperature to 350 degrees. Bake for 30 to 35 minutes or until knife inserted between center and edge comes out clean. Cool. Garnish with sweetened whipped cream and slivered almonds.

Nora Westman
Eugene, Oregon

SWEET POTATO-RAISIN PIES

2 c. mashed cooked sweet potatoes
1 stick margarine, softened
4 eggs
2 c. sugar
1 1/2 c. raisins
2 1/2 tsp. cinnamon
1/2 tsp. ginger
1/2 tsp. nutmeg
2 unbaked pie shells

Combine sweet potatoes, margarine, eggs, sugar, raisins and spices in bowl; mix well. Pour into pie shells. Bake at 350 degrees for 35 to 40 minutes or until set.

Michael L. Brodie
Shamrock, Texas

TANGERINE CHIFFON PIE

1 env. unflavored gelatin
Sugar
Dash of salt
4 eggs, separated
1/4 c. fresh lemon juice
1 c. tangerine juice

1 tbsp. grated tangerine rind
1 baked 9-in. pie shell
3 tbsp. orange liqueur
1 c. heavy cream, whipped
2 tangerines, peeled, sectioned

Combine gelatin, 1/2 cup sugar and salt in double boiler. Beat in egg yolks, lemon and tangerine juices. Cook over boiling water until sugar and gelatin are dissolved and mixture thickens, stirring constantly. Stir in tangerine rind. Chill until partially set. Beat egg whites with 1/3 cup sugar until stiff. Fold into custard. Spoon into pie shell. Chill for 3 hours or longer. Blend liqueur into whipped cream. Spread over pie. Top with tangerine sections.

Doreen Kirk
Doniphan, Missouri

ELEGANT TANGERINE PIE

1 c. fresh tangerine juice
2 tbsp. grated tangerine rind
3 tbsp. flour
2 tbsp. fresh lemon juice
1/2 tsp. grated orange rind
1/2 c. sugar
3 eggs, separated
1 baked 9-in. pie shell

Blend first 6 ingredients with beaten egg yolks in double boiler. Cook over hot water until thick, stirring constantly; cool. Fold in stiffly beaten egg whites. Spoon into pie shell. Bake at 400 degrees for 10 minutes.

Prue Bryson
Tifton, Georgia

TIA MARIA PIE

1/2 lb. butter, softened
2 c. confectioners' sugar
1 tbsp. cocoa
1 tsp. instant coffee powder
3 eggs
1/4 tsp. Tia Maria liqueur
1 9-in. graham cracker pie shell

Combine first 6 ingredients in bowl; blend well. Spoon into pie shell. Freeze, covered, until firm. Garnish with whipped cream.

Nancy Smith
Casa Grande, Arizona

TUTTI FRUTTI PIE

1 1/2 c. drained pineapple tidbits
1 c. chopped pecans
1/2 c. shredded coconut
1/4 c. chopped maraschino cherries
1 1/2 c. chopped dates
2 c. cornflakes
3 eggs, beaten
1/2 c. sugar
1/2 tsp. salt
1 tsp. vanilla extract
1 unbaked 9-in. pie shell

Combine first 6 ingredients in bowl; mix well. Beat eggs until thick and lemon colored. Blend in sugar, salt and vanilla. Stir into pineapple mixture. Spoon into pie shell. Bake at 450 degrees for 10 minutes. Reduce temperature to 350 degrees. Bake for 20 to 30 minutes longer or until lightly browned.

Bonita Landrum
Mobile, Alabama

BLACK WALNUT PIE

3/4 c. sugar
3 eggs
1 tbsp. flour
1 c. corn syrup
1 tsp. vanilla extract
1/4 c. butter, melted
1 c. black walnuts
1 unbaked 9-in. pie shell

Combine first 7 ingredients in bowl; mix well. Pour into pie shell. Bake at 350 degrees until knife inserted in center comes out clean.

Sally Friesen
Bowling Green, Ohio

FRENCH WALNUT PIE

1 c. sugar
1/2 c. margarine, softened
1/4 c. sweetened condensed milk
1 tsp. vanilla extract
1 c. chopped walnuts
1 c. raisins
2 eggs, beaten
1 unbaked 9-in. pie shell

Cream sugar and margarine in large bowl. Stir in condensed milk, vanilla, walnuts and raisins. Fold eggs into creamed mixture. Pour into pie shell. Bake at 325 degrees for 1 hour. Serve with whipped cream or vanilla ice cream.

Carol Winter
Bountiful, Utah

WALNUT-RUM PIE

3 eggs, slightly beaten
1/2 c. sugar
1/4 tsp. salt
1 c. dark corn syrup
3 tbsp. rum
1 c. coarsely chopped walnuts
1 unbaked 9-in. pie shell

Combine first 6 ingredients in bowl; mix well. Pour into pie shell. Bake at 325 degrees for 50 minutes. Garnish with whipped cream.

Stacy Morehead
Owenton, Kentucky

WATERMELON SPICE PIE

Watermelon rind
1 c. sugar
1 tsp. cinnamon
1/3 tsp. nutmeg
1/4 tsp. cloves
1/8 tsp. salt
2 tbsp. flour
1/4 c. vinegar
1/2 c. raisins
1 recipe 2-crust pie pastry

Cut green outer rind and most of pulp from watermelon rind; cut into 1/4-inch cubes. Combine 1 1/2 cups cubes with water to cover in saucepan. Simmer until tender. Drain; add sugar, cinnamon, nutmeg, cloves, salt, flour, vinegar and raisins; mix well. Pour into pastry-lined 8-inch pie plate. Top with remaining pastry; seal edge and cut vents. Bake at 450 degrees until browned. Reduce temperature to 350 degrees. Bake until filling is set.

Thomasina Terry
Hershey, Pennsylvania

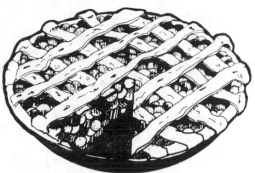

PERFECT
PIE CRUSTS

PROPORTIONS FOR BASIC ROLLED PIE PASTRY

	1-Crust 8 or 9-Inch	1-Crust 10-Inch	2-Crust 8 or 9-Inch	2-Crust 10-Inch
Flour	1 c.	1 1/2 c.	2 c.	3 c.
Salt	1/2 tsp.	3/4 tsp.	1 tsp.	1 1/2 tsp.
Shortening	1/3 c.	1/2 c.	2/3 c.	1 c.
Water	2 tbsp.	3 tbsp.	4 tbsp.	6 tbsp.

VARIATIONS FOR TOP CRUSTS

1/2 recipe 2-crust pie pastry

Shape dough into 1-inch roll. Chill for several hours. Cut into thin slices. Arrange overlapping slices in circle of desired size on baking sheet.

Roll dough on lightly floured surface to desired thickness. Cut with cookie cutters such as star or scalloped round; cut round into quarters to make wedges. Place on baking sheet.

Roll dough on lightly floured surface. Cut out small design from center of circle. Fold under outside edge to smaller diameter than pie plate; flute edge. Place on baking sheet.

Brush dough with cream, melted butter or beaten egg. Bake at 425 degrees until brown; cool slightly before removing to wire rack to cool completely. Top prepared pie with baked pastry.

LATTICE-TOPPED PIE

1/2 recipe 2-crust pie pastry

Roll dough on lightly floured surface. Cut into ten 1/2-inch wide strips. Fill pastry-lined pie plate with filling. Moisten edge of bottom crust with milk or water. Arrange half the strips horizontally over top pressing ends securely to bottom crust. Arrange remaining strips perpendic-ular to first strips, pressing ends tightly. Flute edge of pie. Brush with milk; sprinkle lightly with sugar. Bake as filling recipe directs.

BLIND-BAKED PIE SHELLS

There are several ways to bake a pie shell which does not contain filling that will reduce shrinkage during baking.

Roll chilled dough 1/8 inch thick on lightly floured surface. Fit over inverted pie plate; prick with fork. Bake at 450 degrees for 10 to 12 minutes. Lift shell from pie plate carefully; place inside plate. Bake for 5 minutes longer.

Fit dough into pie plate as usual. Place second pan on dough; weight with rice or dried beans. Bake at 450 degrees for 12 minutes; remove top pan. Bake for 5 minutes longer.

BOILING WATER PASTRIES

2/3 c. shortening
2 c. sifted flour
1 tsp. salt

Place shortening in bowl. Add 1/3 cup boiling water gradually, mixing with fork. Add flour and salt; mix well. Divide into 2 portions. Roll on floured surface.

Ava Finney
Steubenville, Ohio

EASY PASTRIES

2 c. flour
1/2 tsp. salt
1/2 c. shortening

Combine flour and salt in bowl. Cut in shortening until crumbly. Sprinkle about 1/4 cup cold water over flour 1 tablespoon at a time; toss lightly to mix. Divide into 2 portions. Roll between waxed paper.

Myrna Johnson
Ashland, Kentucky

FLAKY PASTRIES

2 c. flour
1 tsp. salt
2/3 c. shortening
2 tbsp. butter
1 tbsp. vinegar

Sift flour and salt into bowl. Cut in shortening and butter until crumbly. Mix vinegar with 5 tablespoons cold water. Add to flour mixture. Stir with fork until dough clings together. Divide into 2 portions. Roll on floured surface.

Sara Palmer
Ft. Wayne, Indiana

PASTRY FOR ONE-CRUST PIE

1 1/2 c. flour
3/4 tsp. salt
1/2 c. shortening

Combine flour and salt in bowl. Cut in shortening until crumbly. Add 3 to 4 tablespoons cold water, 1 tablespoon at a time, tossing lightly to mix. Shape into ball. Let stand for 5 minutes before rolling.

Rosemary Paul
Louisville, Kentucky

SURE-FIRE PASTRY

1 1/2 c. sifted flour
1/2 tsp. salt
1/2 c. shortening

Sift flour and salt into bowl. Reserve 1/4 cup mixture. Cut shortening into remaining flour until crumbly. Combine reserved flour and 3 tablespoons water to make smooth paste. Stir paste into shortening mixture. Shape into ball. Roll on floured surface.

Miriam Renick
Davenport, Iowa

MAKE-AHEAD PIE PASTRIES

5 c. flour
1 1/2 tsp. salt
2 1/4 c. shortening
1 egg, beaten
2 tbsp. white vinegar

Combine flour and salt in large bowl. Cut in shortening until crumbly. Beat egg with 1 cup cold water and vinegar. Stir into flour mixture with fork gradually. Divide into 3 portions. Store, wrapped tightly, in refrigerator.

Judith Burton
Medinah, Minnesota

NEVER-FAIL PIE CRUSTS

3 c. sifted flour
3/4 tsp. salt
1 c. shortening
1 egg, well beaten
1 tsp. vinegar

Combine flour and salt in bowl. Cut in shortening until crumbly. Stir egg mixed with vinegar and 5 tablespoons cold water into flour mixture. Divide into 4 portions. Store, tightly wrapped, in refrigerator.

Dorothy Masters
Moline, Illinois

THREE PIE SHELLS

4 c. flour
1 tbsp. sugar
2 3/4 c. shortening
1 tbsp. vinegar
1 egg, beaten

Combine flour and sugar in bowl. Cut in shortening until crumbly. Add vinegar, egg and 1/2 cup water; mix well. Knead lightly on floured surface. Roll and fit into 3 pie plates.

Irene Edwards
Milwaukee, Wisconsin

GOLDEN PIE SHELL

1 1/4 c. sifted flour
1/2 tsp. salt
3/8 c. margarine
1 egg, beaten

Sift flour and salt into bowl. Cut in margarine until crumbly. Add egg; toss to mix, adding a small amount of water if necessary. Roll between waxed paper.

Diana Russell
Tucson, Arizona

PENNSYLVANIA DUTCH PASTRY

3 c. flour
1 tsp. salt
1 1/4 c. shortening
1 egg, beaten
1 tsp. vinegar

Sift flour and salt into bowl. Cut in shortening until crumbly. Beat egg with vinegar and 5 tablespoons cold water. Add to flour mixture; mix well. Chill, wrapped, for several hours.

Shirley Chandler
Clayton, Missouri

RICH PASTRY FOR EIGHT PIE SHELLS

5 c. sifted flour
1 tsp. baking powder
1 1/2 tsp. salt
3 tbsp. packed brown sugar
2 1/2 c. shortening
1 egg, beaten
2 tbsp. vinegar

Sift flour, baking powder, salt and sugar into large bowl. Cut in shortening until crumbly. Add enough water to egg to measure 3/4 cup; stir in vinegar. Pour over flour mixture; toss until moistened. Divide into 8 portions. Wrap in foil. Store in freezer. Thaw overnight in refrigerator.

Florence Evans
Flushing, New York

EASY BUTTER PASTRIES

1 3/4 c. sifted flour
1 tbsp. sugar
1/4 tsp. salt
1/2 c. butter

Sift flour, sugar and salt into bowl. Cut in butter until crumbly. Sprinkle 4 to 6 tablespoons cold water, 1 teaspoon at a time, over flour; toss lightly with fork to mix. Shape into 2 portions. Store, tightly wrapped, in refrigerator until ready to use.

Marilyn McCoy
Bennington, Vermont

RICH BUTTER PASTRY

2 c. flour
1/2 tsp. salt
1/3 tsp. baking powder
1/3 c. shortening
1/3 c. butter

Mix first 3 ingredients in bowl. Cut in shortening until crumbly. Mix in 5 to 6 tablespoons ice water to make dough. Roll into rectangle on lightly floured surface. Dot with 1/3 of the butter; roll as for jelly roll. Roll into rectangle. Dot with half the remaining butter; roll as for jelly roll. Repeat. Wrap in waxed paper. Chill for 2 hours or longer.

Emma Gould
Wheaton, Illinois

ONE WHOLE WHEAT PIE SHELL

1 1/4 c. whole wheat flour
1/2 tsp. salt
1/2 c. shortening

Combine flour and salt in bowl. Cut in shortening until crumbly. Add enough cold water to make dough; mix well. Roll 1/8 inch thick on floured surface. Fit into pie plate; prick with fork. Bake at 450 degrees for 12 minutes.

Vivian Sidney
Glenview, Illinois

MAKE-AHEAD WHOLE WHEAT PIE SHELLS

1 c. whole wheat flour
1 c. sifted all-purpose flour
1 tsp. salt
1/2 to 2/3 c. shortening

Stir flours and salt together into bowl. Cut in shortening until crumbly. Stir 4 to 5 tablespoons water into mixture to make soft dough. Chill, wrapped in waxed paper, for 2 hours or longer. Divide into 2 portions. Roll 1/4 inch thick on floured surface. Fit into 8-inch pie plates; prick shells with fork. Bake at 425 degrees for 10 minutes. Reduce temperature to 350 degrees. Bake for 10 minutes longer.

Anne Bishop
Ardmore, Oklahoma

OATMEAL PIE SHELL

3/4 c. sifted flour
1/2 tsp. salt
1/3 c. shortening
1/2 c. oats

Sift flour and salt into bowl. Cut in shortening until crumbly. Stir in oats. Mix in 3 tablespoons water gradually. Shape into ball. Roll into 13-inch circle on floured surface. Fit into 9-inch pie plate.

Terry Burke
Grand Island, Nebraska

CHICKEN FAT PASTRY

2 1/4 c. sifted flour
3/4 tsp. salt
3/4 c. chicken fat, chilled
6 tbsp. milk

Combine flour and salt in bowl. Cut in fat. Add milk gradually; mix lightly with fork until moistened. Shape into ball. Chill, covered, for several minutes. Roll on floured surface.

Rita Drake
Youngstown, Ohio

BEST-EVER PIE CRUST

2 c. lard, melted
4 c. flour
1 c. milk
2 tsp. salt

Combine all ingredients in bowl; mix well. Dough will be soft. Store, tightly covered, in refrigerator overnight or up to 2 weeks.

Lillian Lindsay
Belleville, Illinois

CRUST FOR MANY PIES

6 c. flour
1/4 c. sugar
1 tbsp. salt
1 lb. lard
2 eggs, beaten
2 tsp. vinegar

Mix first 3 ingredients in bowl. Cut in lard until crumbly. Beat eggs with vinegar and 10 tablespoons water. Sprinkle over flour mixture; toss lightly with fork to mix. Chill, tightly covered, for 2 hours. Pastry will keep for 2 to 3 weeks.

Bea Lockwood
Patterson, New Jersey

SPECIAL PIE CRUSTS

1 egg, beaten
1 tbsp. vinegar
5 1/2 c. flour
2 tbsp. brown sugar
1 tsp. baking powder
1 tbsp. salt
1 lb. lard

Add enough cold water to egg to measure 3/4 cup; mix in vinegar. Mix flour with brown sugar, baking powder and salt in bowl. Cut in lard until crumbly. Add egg mixture all at once; mix well. Store, covered, in refrigerator.

Claire Blackmon
Del Monte, California

FIFTEEN-MINUTE PASTRY MIX

8 c. sifted flour
2 tsp. salt
2 c. shortening

Sift flour and salt into bowl. Cut in shortening until crumbly. For 1 crust: Mix 1 1/2 cups mixture with 3 tablespoons flour blended with 3 tablespoons water. For 2 crusts: Mix 2 cups mixture with mixture of 1/4 cup flour and 1/4 cup water. Store unused mixture and scraps of leftover pastry tightly wrapped in refrigerator. Let stand at room temperature before using.

Christy Flynn
Pinehurst, North Carolina

TWO-CRUST OIL PASTRY

2 c. sifted flour
3/4 tsp. salt
1 tsp. baking powder
1/2 c. oil

Sift flour with salt and baking powder into large bowl. Whip salad oil with 6 tablespoons ice water in small bowl. Stir into flour mixture. Divide into 2 portions. Roll on floured surface.

Meredith Thompson
San Antonio, Texas

PERFECT PASTRY MIX

6 c. sifted flour
1 tbsp. salt
2 c. shortening

Sift flour and salt into bowl. Cut in shortening until crumbly. Store in covered bowl in refrigerator for 1 month or less. Toss with fork to lighten before measuring. Mix 1/4 cup pastry mix with 2 to 3 tablespoons cold water for each 9-inch crust.

Gwen Schofield
Enid, Oklahoma

CRUST FOR FRIED PIES

5 c. flour
1 tsp. baking powder
1 tsp. salt
1 tsp. sugar
1 c. shortening
1 lg. can evaporated milk
1 egg, slightly beaten

Sift dry ingredients together in bowl. Cut in shortening until crumbly. Combine remaining ingredients. Stir into dry ingredients; mix well. Roll on floured surface; cut as desired. Fill with favorite filling; seal well. Fry in hot deep fat until golden brown.

Katy Ball
Pierre, South Dakota

EASY CORNFLAKE PIE CRUST

1 1/2 c. crushed cornflakes
1/3 c. butter, softened
2 tbsp. sugar
1/8 tsp. nutmeg

Combine all ingredients in bowl; mix well. Press over bottom and side of 7-inch pie plate. Chill until firm. May bake at 350 degrees for 10 minutes.

Radene Craig
Jefferson City, Missouri

CRUNCHY CHOCOLATE PIE CRUST

1 c. semisweet chocolate chips
3 tbsp. butter or margarine
2 c. cornflakes

Melt chips and butter in double boiler. Add cornflakes; mix well. Press over bottom and side of 9-inch pie plate. Chill until firm.

Harriet Dillard
Ardmore, Oklahoma

CORNFLAKE-COCONUT CRUST

3/4 c. cornflake crumbs
2 tbsp. flaked coconut
2 tbsp. sugar
1/4 c. butter, softened

Combine all ingredients in bowl; mix well. Press over bottom and side of 8-inch pie pan. Chill until firm.

Jessie Morrow
Alexandria, Louisiana

CRISPY CRUST

1/4 c. corn syrup
2 tbsp. brown sugar
3 tbsp. margarine
2 1/2 c. crispy rice cereal

Combine corn syrup, brown sugar and margarine in medium saucepan. Bring to a boil over low heat, stirring constantly. Remove from heat. Add cereal; stir until well coated. Press evenly into 9-inch pie pan. Chill until firm.

Annette Grover
Fallon, Nevada

CRUNCHY FROZEN CRUST

1 1/4 c. Rice Chex, finely crushed
1/2 c. packed brown sugar
1/2 c. flaked coconut
1/4 c. chopped pecans
1/2 stick butter, melted

Combine all ingredients in bowl; mix well. Reserve 1/4 of the mixture for topping if desired. Press remaining mixture over bottom and side of 9-inch pie plate. Freeze until firm.

Alice Green
Modesto, California

FAVORITE CRUMB PIE SHELL

2 1/3 c. sugar-coated cornflakes, crushed
6 graham crackers, crushed
1/4 c. butter, melted

Combine crumbs in bowl. Add butter; mix well. Press over bottom and side of 9-inch pie plate. Bake at 375 degrees for 8 minutes.

Livinia Carr
Allentown, Pennsylvania

EASY CHOCOLATE CRUMB CRUST

1 pkg. chocolate wafers
1/2 tsp. cinnamon
1/2 c. melted butter

Process wafers in blender to make very fine crumbs. Mix crumbs, cinnamon and butter in bowl. Press firmly over bottom and side of 9-inch pie plate. Chill until firm.

Lou Dundee
Boise, Idaho

COCONUT-GINGERSNAP CRUST

1 3 1/2-oz. can flaked coconut
2 tbsp. melted butter
2 tbsp. sugar
1/4 c. fine gingersnap crumbs

Combine all ingredients in bowl; mix well. Press over bottom and side of 8-inch pie plate. Bake at 375 degrees for 10 minutes.

Honey Goodrich
Oak Park, Illinois

BASIC GRAHAM CRACKER CRUST

1 1/4 c. fine graham cracker crumbs
3 tbsp. sugar
1/3 to 1/2 c. butter, softened

Combine all ingredients in bowl; mix well. Add 1 to 2 tablespoons water or enough to blend mixture. Press over bottom and side of 9-inch pie plate. Bake at 350 degrees for 10 minutes.

Ernestine Garrett
Green Bay, Wisconsin

CHOCOLATE GRAHAM CRACKER CRUST

1 pkg. graham crackers
1/4 c. confectioners' sugar
1/4 tsp. nutmeg
1/4 tsp. cinnamon
1 tbsp. cocoa
1/4 c. melted margarine

Process graham crackers, several at a time, in blender to make fine crumbs. Combine with remaining dry ingredients in bowl; mix well. Stir in margarine gradually. Press over bottom and side of 9-inch pie plate. Chill until firm.

Jimmy Lee Smith
Chadron, Nebraska

WALNUT CRUMB SHELL

1 c. graham cracker crumbs
2/3 c. finely chopped walnuts
1/4 c. melted butter
1 egg white, beaten

Mix crumbs and walnuts in bowl; stir in butter and egg white. Press over bottom and side of 9-inch pie plate. Bake at 350 degrees for 10 to 12 minutes or until brown; cool.

Beth Dawkins
Fort Scott, Kansas

MICROWAVE CRUMB PIE SHELL

1/4 c. butter
1 1/4 c. fine chocolate, vanilla, lemon,
*   gingersnap or macaroon cookie crumbs*
2 tbsp. sugar

Microwave butter in glass pie plate for 1 1/2 minutes or until bubbly. Combine crumbs with sugar; stir into butter. Press over bottom and side of 9-inch pie plate. Microwave for 2 to 2 1/2 minutes or until firm, turning once.

Freddie Singer
Cheboygan, Michigan

COFFEE CRUMB CRUST

1 1/3 c. vanilla or chocolate wafer crumbs
2 tsp. instant coffee powder
1/4 c. sugar
1/4 c. butter, softened

Mix first 3 ingredients in bowl. Cut in butter until crumbly. Press over bottom and side of pie plate. Bake at 325 degrees for 10 minutes.

Alana Sinkwich
Joplin, Missouri

VANILLA WAFER CRUMB CRUST

1 1/2 c. fine vanilla wafer crumbs
1/4 c. butter, softened

Mix crumbs with butter in bowl. Press over bottom and side of 9-inch pie plate. Bake at 375 degrees for 8 minutes. May substitute chocolate wafers or gingersnaps for vanilla wafers, adding sugar to taste.

Virginia Akins
Hamilton, Ohio

ZWIEBACK-CINNAMON CRUST

18 Zwieback, crumbled
1 tsp. cinnamon
1/2 c. sugar
4 tbsp. butter

Combine crumbs, cinnamon and sugar in bowl. Cut in butter until crumbly. Reserve 1/4 of the crumbs for topping if desired; press remaining crumbs into 9-inch pie plate.

Henny Armstrong
Atlantic City, New Jersey

ZWIEBACK-PECAN CRUST

1 c. fine Zwieback crumbs
1 c. ground pecans
2/3 c. sugar
1/4 tsp. cinnamon
1/2 c. butter, melted

Combine crumbs, pecans, sugar and cinnamon in bowl. Reserve 1/2 cup crumb mixture for topping if desired. Add butter to remaining mixture; mix well. Press into 10-inch pie pan. Chill until set.

Addie Paul
Augusta, Maine

FAVORITE CHEDDAR CHEESE PIE CRUST

2 c. sifted flour
1/2 tsp. salt
1 c. grated sharp Cheddar cheese
1/2 c. shortening

Sift flour with salt into bowl. Add cheese; toss to mix. Cut in shortening until crumbly. Add 3 to 4 tablespoons cold water gradually, mixing to make dough. Roll out on floured surface.

Angela Buxton
Poplar Bluff, Missouri

ONE-CRUST CHEDDAR CHEESE PASTRY

1 c. flour
1/2 tsp. salt
1/2 c. shredded Cheddar cheese
1/3 c. shortening

Sift flour and salt into bowl. Add cheese; toss to mix. Cut in shortening until crumbly. Sprinkle with 3 to 4 tablespoons cold water, tossing lightly with fork. Roll out on lightly floured surface.

Alpha Jean Hart
Trinidad, Colorado

CRISP AND DRY MERINGUE PIE SHELL

4 egg whites
1/2 tsp. cream of tartar
1 c. sugar

Beat egg whites until foamy. Add cream of tartar; beat until soft peaks form. Add sugar gradually, beating constantly, until stiff. Spread 1 inch thick over bottom of 9-inch pie plate. Spread remaining meringue over side of pie plate, building up edge. Bake at 250 degrees for 2 hours and 15 minutes or until dry. Cool on wire rack. Store in airtight container.

Doris Janowicz
Wausau, Wisconsin

COCONUT-WALNUT MERINGUE CRUST

4 egg whites
1/8 tsp. salt

1 tsp. vanilla extract
1 c. sugar
1 c. graham cracker crumbs
1/2 c. chopped moist coconut
1/2 c. chopped walnuts

Beat egg whites with salt and vanilla until soft peaks form. Add sugar gradually, beating until stiff. Combine crumbs, coconut and walnuts. Fold into stiffly beaten egg whites. Spread in greased 9-inch pie plate. Bake at 350 degrees for 30 minutes.

Babette Lunn
Tupelo, Mississippi

CHOCOLATE-COCONUT MERINGUE CRUST

3 egg whites, stiffly beaten
1/3 tsp. cream of tartar
1 c. sugar
1 tsp. vanilla extract
1 c. chopped nuts
18 soda crackers, crushed

Combine stiffly beaten egg whites and cream of tartar in bowl. Add sugar gradually, beating until very stiff. Fold in vanilla, nuts and crumbs. Spread in greased 9-inch pie plate. Bake at 325 degrees for 35 minutes.

Geraldine Cannon
Shreveport, Louisiana

BASIC CHEESE PASTRY

1 c. flour
1/4 tsp. salt
1/3 c. shortening
1/4 c. grated sharp cheese

Mix flour and salt in bowl. Cut in shortening until crumbly. Add cheese; mix well. Add 2 tablespoons ice water; toss to mix. Shape into ball. Chill thoroughly before rolling on floured surface.

Alicia Brough
Cordova, Arkansas

GOOD CREAM CHEESE PASTRY

2 c. sifted flour
1/2 tsp. salt

2/3 c. butter
12 oz. cream cheese

Mix flour and salt in bowl. Cut in butter and cream cheese until crumbly. Press into firm ball. Smooth edges. Chill for 30 minutes or until firm enough to roll.

Lesley Fry
Irvington, New Jersey

DELUXE CREAM CHEESE PASTRY

1 c. butter, softened
1 8-oz. package cream cheese, softened
1/2 tsp. salt
2 c. flour

Combine butter, cream cheese and salt in mixer bowl; beat until thoroughly blended. Work in flour with fingertips; shape into ball. Wrap tightly. Chill overnight. Let stand at room temperature for 10 minutes before rolling.

Tracy Freedrich
Ogden, Utah

FAVORITE CREAM CHEESE PASTRY

1/2 c. butter
1 3-oz. package cream cheese, softened
1 1/2 c. sifted cake flour
1/8 tsp. salt

Beat butter and cream cheese together in bowl. Add flour and salt; blend well. Chill, covered, for 1 hour or longer. Roll 1/8 inch thick on floured surface. Fit into pie plate; prick with fork. Bake at 375 degrees for 10 to 15 minutes.

Rose Betz
Reading, Pennsylvania

MOTHER'S PIE CRUST

1 tsp. sugar
1/2 tsp. salt
1/2 c. oil
2 c. flour

Combine first 3 ingredients with 5 tablespoons water in bowl; mix well. Add flour; mix well. Press into pie plate.

Julie Anthony
Omaha, Nebraska

CANDY PIE SHELL

2/3 c. semisweet chocolate chips
1/4 c. butter
1/4 c. milk
2 cans flaked coconut

Combine first 3 ingredients in small saucepan. Cook over low heat until chocolate melts, blending well. Fold in coconut. Spread over bottom and side of greased 9-inch pie plate. Chill until firm.

Glenda Palmer
Redding, California

DIFFERENT CHOCOLATE-COCONUT PIE SHELL

2 sq. chocolate, melted
3 tbsp. butter, melted
1 tsp. vanilla extract
1/4 c. sweetened condensed milk
1/2 c. sifted confectioners' sugar
2 c. flaked coconut

Blend first 4 ingredients in bowl. Add confectioners' sugar; blend well. Stir in coconut until coated. Press over bottom and side of 9-inch pie plate. Wrap tightly. Chill for 1 hour or until firm.

Maxine Westland
New Haven, Connecticut

COCONUT-NUT CRUST

1 5-oz. package shredded coconut
1/3 c. chopped nuts
5 tbsp. melted butter

Combine all ingredients in blender container. Process until well mixed. Press over bottom and side of 9-inch pie plate. Bake at 325 degrees for 10 minutes. Cool.

Calene Patterson
Casper, Wyoming

COCONUT-PECAN CRUST WITH LEMON CHEESECAKE FILLING

1 3 1/2-oz. can flaked coconut
Chopped pecans
2 tbsp. butter, melted

COCONUT-PECAN CRUST WITH
LEMON CHEESECAKE FILLING

2 c. cottage cheese
2 sm. packages lemon instant pudding mix
1 3/4 c. milk
2 tbsp. grated lemon rind
1/2 c. sour cream

Combine coconut, 1/4 cup pecans and butter in small bowl; mix well. Press over bottom and side of 9-inch pie plate. Bake at 325 degrees for 15 to 20 minutes or until golden brown. Cool. Beat cottage cheese in small bowl until smooth. Prepare pudding mix according to package directions using 1 3/4 cups milk. Stir in cottage cheese and lemon rind. Turn into pie shell. Top with sour cream and additional pecans. Chill for several hours.

Photograph for this recipe above.

CONFECTIONERS' SUGAR CRUST

1 c. flour
2 tbsp. confectioners' sugar
3/8 c. melted margarine

Combine flour and sugar in bowl. Add margarine; blend well with fork. Press over bottom and side of 9-inch pie pan. Bake at 250 degrees until golden brown.

Marlene Towson
Worcester, Massachusetts

CAKE MIX PIE CRUST

1 pkg. white cake mix
1 c. quick-cooking oats
6 tbsp. butter, softened
1 egg

Combine cake mix, oats and butter in large mixer bowl. Beat at low speed until crumbly. Reserve 1 cup crumbs for topping if desired. Mix remaining crumb mixture with egg. Press over bottom and side of 10-inch pie plate. Bake at 350 degrees for 12 minutes.

Edith Callet
Pendleton, Oregon

DUTCH BUTTER CRUST

1/2 c. butter, softened
1 c. sugar
1 1/2 c. sifted flour
1 tsp. cinnamon
1/2 tsp. each baking powder, salt
1/4 tsp. nutmeg

Cream butter and sugar in small bowl. Sift dry ingredients into creamed mixture gradually; mix well. Reserve 1 cup for topping, if desired. Press remaining mixture over bottom and side of 8-inch pie plate. Spoon in filling. Bake using filling directions.

Babe Mann
Tulsa, Oklahoma

SWEET NUTTY CRUST

1 c. flour
1/4 c. chopped nuts
1/2 c. confectioners' sugar
1 stick margarine, melted

Combine first 3 ingredients in bowl; mix well. Add margarine; mix well. Press over bottom and side of large pie plate. Bake at 350 degrees until lightly browned.

Jaqueline Suggs
Springfield, New Jersey

RICH SWEET PIE SHELLS

1 1/2 c. flour
3 tbsp. sugar
3/4 c. margarine, softened
Pinch of salt

Combine all ingredients in bowl; mix well. Press into two 8-inch pie plates. Bake at 250 degrees for 20 minutes.

LouAnn Siler
Crestville, Georgia

SAUCEPAN CRUST

1/2 c. butter
1 tbsp. sugar
1 c. flour

Melt butter and sugar in saucepan. Add flour; stir until mixture forms ball. Press over bottom and side of 9-inch pie plate, shaping edge. Spoon in filling. Bake using filling directions.

Sandy Cohen
Cuyahoga Falls, Ohio

SWEET PECAN PIE CRUST

1/2 c. margarine
1 1/4 c. flour
1/2 c. chopped pecans
2 tbsp. light corn syrup

Melt margarine in saucepan; blend in flour. Add pecans and corn syrup. Cook over medium heat for 3 to 4 minutes or until mixture begins to brown, stirring constantly. Reserve 1/3 cup for topping, if desired. Press remaining pecan mixture over bottom and side of 9-inch pie pan. Cool.

Helaine Newell
Pasadena, California

COCOA PIE SHELL

1 1/2 c. sifted flour
1/2 tsp. salt
2 tbsp. cocoa
1/2 c. shortening

Mix first 3 ingredients in bowl. Cut in shortening until crumbly. Sprinkle 3 tablespoons cold water over mixture; mix lightly until dough forms a ball. Roll between 2 sheets of waxed paper. Fit pastry into pie plate; prick with fork. Bake at 450 degrees for 10 to 12 minutes.

Dawn Kalber
Norfolk, Nebraska

CHOCOLATE-BLACK WALNUT CRUST

1 c. flour
1/4 c. packed light brown sugar
1/2 tsp. salt
1 tsp. oats
1/3 c. coarsely chopped black walnuts
1/3 c. butter, chilled
1 sq. unsweetened chocolate, grated
1 tsp. vanilla extract

Sift flour, brown sugar and salt into bowl. Add oats, walnuts, butter and chocolate; mix well. Add vanilla and 1 tablespoon ice water; mix until ingredients hold together. Roll between waxed paper. Pat into 9-inch pie pan. Prick all over with fork. Bake at 350 degrees for 20 minutes or until light brown.

Susie Mills
Durham, North Carolina

CHOCOLATE-ORANGE PIE SHELL

1 c. flour
Pinch of salt
2 tbsp. cocoa
2 tbsp. sugar
Grated rind of 1 orange
Butter
1 egg yolk

Combine dry ingredients in bowl. Cut in 6 1/3 tablespoons butter. Mix in egg yolk. Roll 1 inch thick on floured surface. Press into 9-inch pie plate. Chill for 15 minutes. Bake at 325 degrees for 25 to 30 minutes or until browned.

Edie Tolan
Flint, Michigan

GINGER ALE PIE SHELL

1 c. sifted flour
1/2 tsp. salt
1/3 c. lard
2 tbsp. (about) ginger ale

Sift flour and salt into bowl. Cut in lard until crumbly. Sprinkle in ginger ale, 1 tablespoon at a time; mix lightly until moistened. Shape into ball. Let rest for several minutes. Roll on floured surface. Fit into 8-inch pie pan. Prick with fork. Bake at 450 degrees for 12 to 15 minutes or until golden brown.

Ada Lock
Presque Isle, Maine

DELICIOUS LEMON CRUST

1 1/2 c. sifted flour
1 tsp. salt
1/2 c. shortening
4 tbsp. lemon juice
1 egg yolk, beaten

Combine flour and salt in bowl. Cut in shortening until crumbly. Beat lemon juice and egg yolk together. Stir into flour mixture to make dough. Roll on lightly floured surface. Fit into 9-inch pie plate. Spoon in favorite fruit filling. Bake using filling directions.

Jeanne Bunch
Deshler, Ohio

MAKE-AHEAD LEMON PASTRY

2 c. flour
1/2 tsp. salt
1/2 to 2/3 c. shortening
1 tsp. grated lemon rind
2 1/2 to 3 tbsp. lemon juice

Mix flour and salt in bowl. Cut in shortening and lemon rind until crumbly. Mix lemon juice with equal amount ice water. Add enough lemon juice mixture to flour mixture to make dough. Chill, wrapped, for 2 hours or longer.

Wanda Massey
Orlando, Florida

SPICY ALMOND PIE PASTRY

4 c. flour
2 c. sugar
1/2 tsp. cinnamon
1/2 tsp. baking powder
1/4 tsp. cloves
1 lb. almonds, ground
1 lb. butter
1 egg, lightly beaten

Sift first 5 ingredients into large bowl; add almonds. Cut in butter until crumbly; mix in egg. Knead lightly; shape into ball. Chill for several minutes before rolling on lightly floured surface. Yield: Two 2-crust pie pastries.

Beverly Osburn
Pueblo, Colorado

MAKE-AHEAD NUT PASTRY

1 1/2 c. flour
1/2 c. finely ground nuts
3/4 tsp. salt
1/2 to 2/3 c. shortening

Mix first 3 ingredients in bowl. Cut in shortening until crumbly. Sprinkle with 5 to 6 tablespoons ice water; mix to make dough. Chill for 2 hours or longer.

Martha Eames
Montclair, New Jersey

TOASTED COCONUT CRUST

1 c. flour
1/2 tsp. salt
1/3 c. shortening
1/2 c. flaked coconut, toasted
3 tbsp. (about) milk

Mix flour and salt in bowl. Cut in shortening until crumbly. Stir in coconut. Mix in enough milk to make dough. Roll out between waxed paper. Fit into pie plate. Bake at 400 degrees for 10 to 12 minutes.

Karen Olsen
Vernal, Utah

EASY PECAN PIE CRUST

1 1/4 c. flour
1/8 tsp. baking powder
1/2 tsp. salt
2 tbsp. ground pecans
1/3 c. shortening

Combine flour, baking powder, salt and pecans in bowl. Cut in shortening until crumbly. Add 2 to 3 tablespoons water, 1 tablespoon at a time; mix until dough holds together. Press into ball.

Knead on lightly floured board for 1 minute. Roll out; fit into 9-inch pie pan. Prick with fork. Bake at 450 degrees for 12 minutes or until golden.

Rosetta Gibson
Pontiac, Michigan

BUTTER-ALMOND PIE SHELLS

1 c. butter
3/4 c. sugar
2 1/3 c. flour
1 c. ground blanched almonds
1 egg, beaten

Combine all ingredients in bowl; mix well. Divide into 2 portions. Roll out thin on floured surface. Fit into 2 buttered pie plates; prick with fork. Bake at 350 degrees for 20 minutes.

Kerry McCullock
Long Beach, California

EASY WALNUT PASTRY

1 c. shortening
2 c. flour
1/2 tsp. salt
1/2 c. finely chopped walnuts

Cut shortening into flour in bowl until crumbly. Add salt, walnuts and 1/2 cup water; mix lightly. Shape into ball. Roll out on floured surface to use.

Fran Wills
Macon, Georgia

ORANGE JUICE PASTRY

1 3/4 c. flour
3/8 c. sugar
Pinch of salt
1/2 c. shortening
1/4 c. orange juice

Sift flour, sugar and salt together. Cut in shortening until crumbly. Sprinkle in orange juice gradually, tossing to make soft dough.

Ruth Faulk
Hutchinson, Kansas

SPECIAL ORANGE PASTRY

3/4 c. butter, softened
2 tbsp. confectioners' sugar
1 egg, separated
2 tsp. grated orange rind
2 c. sifted flour
1/2 tsp. salt
1/4 c. orange juice

Cream butter with confectioners' sugar and egg yolk in bowl. Add orange rind and dry ingredients; mix well. Add orange juice; mix until stiff dough forms. Chill for several minutes. Roll out on floured surface. Brush with slightly beaten egg white.

Breanne Barber
Salisbury, Maryland

SPICY ORANGE PIE SHELL

1 c. sifted flour
2 tbsp. sugar
1/2 tsp. salt
1/4 tsp. cinnamon
1/8 tsp. ginger
1/8 tsp. cloves
1/3 c. shortening
2 1/2 tbsp. (about) orange juice

Sift first 6 ingredients into bowl. Cut in shortening until crumbly. Sprinkle orange juice into mixture 1 teaspoon at a time, tossing to mix. Roll on floured surface to fit 8 or 9-inch pie plate.

Darlene Connolly
Stockton, California

PEANUT BUTTER PIE SHELLS

2 c. flour, sifted
1 tsp. salt
1/3 c. shortening
1/2 c. smooth peanut butter

Sift flour and salt into bowl. Cut in shortening and peanut butter until crumbly. Add 1/3 cup ice water; mix with fork until well moistened. Chill for several minutes. Divide into 2 portions. Roll on floured surface. Fit into two 9-inch pie plates; prick with fork. Bake at 450 degrees for 10 minutes.

Evelyn Hatchkiss
Muncie, Indiana

POPPY SEED PIE SHELL

1 1/3 c. sifted flour
1/2 tsp. salt
1 tbsp. poppy seed
1/2 c. shortening

Combine first 3 ingredients in bowl. Cut in shortening until crumbly. Add 3 tablespoons water; mix lightly. Roll on floured surface. Fit into 9-inch pie plate. Bake at 425 degrees for 12 to 15 minutes or until brown.

Susie LaNalle
Batavia, New York

MICROWAVE SOUR CREAM PIE SHELL

1 1/2 c. flour
3/4 tsp. salt
1/2 c. shortening
3 to 4 tbsp. sour cream

Mix flour and salt in bowl. Cut in shortening until crumbly. Mix in sour cream. Roll between waxed paper. Fit into pie shell; prick with fork. Microwave on Medium for 7 to 9 minutes, giving dish a quarter turn after 4 minutes.

May Mallory
Olympia, Washington

RICH SOUR CREAM PIE CRUST

2 c. flour
1 tsp. baking powder
1/2 tsp. salt
1 tbsp. sugar
1/4 lb. butter, softened
1 egg yolk
3 tbsp. sour cream

Sift first 4 ingredients into bowl. Cut in butter until crumbly. Add egg yolk and sour cream; blend well. Roll into 2 circles on floured surface.

Nelda Emerson
Oakley, Kansas

CAKE MIX TOPPING

1 c. butter, softened
1 sm. package yellow cake mix
1/2 c. flaked coconut

Cut butter into cake mix in bowl until crumbly. Mix in coconut. Sprinkle over pie filling. Bake as filling directs.

Susannah Tucker
De Land, Florida

CHEDDAR CHEESE TOPPING

1/4 c. butter, melted
1/2 c. flour
1/2 c. grated Cheddar cheese
1/4 c. sugar
1/8 tsp. salt

Combine all ingredients in bowl; mix well. Sprinkle over filling. Bake as filling directs.

Patsy Swanson
Fresno, California

CHEESY CRUMB TOPPING

3/4 c. sugar
1/2 tsp. cinnamon
1/2 c. flour
1/2 tsp. salt
1/4 c. shortening
3/4 c. grated cheese

Combine all ingredients in bowl; mix well. Sprinkle over filling. Bake as filling directs.

Monica Stevins
Valdosta, Georgia

CORNFLAKE-WALNUT TOPPING

1/2 c. packed brown sugar
1/2 c. softened margarine
3/4 c. crushed cornflakes
1 c. chopped walnuts

Combine all ingredients in bowl; mix well. Spread over filling. Bake at 400 degrees for 12 to 15 minutes or until brown.

Jane Thornton
Huntsville, Alabama

CRUNCHY NUT TOPPING

1/3 c. peanut butter
1/3 c. margarine
2 1/2 c. quick-cooking oats
1/2 c. packed brown sugar
1/2 c. finely chopped peanuts

Melt peanut butter and margarine in saucepan. Stir in remaining ingredients. Spread on baking sheet. Bake at 350 degrees for 15 to 18 minutes or until golden brown, stirring occasionally. Cool completely before sprinkling over pie. May omit peanut butter, increase margarine to 1/2 cup and substitute pecans for peanuts.

Cynthia Dugan
Grand Forks, North Dakota

GRANOLA TOPPING

2/3 c. packed brown sugar
1/3 c. finely chopped nuts
1 tsp. cinnamon
1/4 c. flour
1 c. granola, crushed

Combine all ingredients in bowl; mix well. Spread in shallow baking dish. Bake at 350 degrees until toasted, stirring frequently. Cool completely. Store in airtight container. Sprinkle over baked pie before serving.

Louise Ward
Middletown, Connecticut

MACAROON TOPPING

1 egg, beaten
1/2 tsp. vanilla extract
1/2 c. biscuit mix
1 tbsp. melted margarine
1/2 c. coconut
1/2 c. sugar

Combine all ingredients in bowl; mix well. Spoon over fruit filling. Bake as filling directs.

Lee Wald
Durango, Colorado

MICROWAVE CRUMB PIE TOPPING

1/3 c. packed brown sugar
1/2 c. flour
1/4 c. butter

Combine brown sugar and flour in bowl. Cut in butter until crumbly. Spread in shallow glass baking dish. Microwave on High for 2 1/2 to 3 minutes or until bubbly, turning twice. Cool slightly; stir with fork. Sprinkle over baked pie.

Blanche Turner
Dahlonega, Florida

NUTTY WHOLE GRAIN TOPPING

1 c. oats
1/2 c. whole wheat flour
3/4 c. packed brown sugar
1/2 c. butter
1/2 c. chopped nuts
1/2 tsp. vanilla extract

Combine oats, flour and brown sugar in bowl. Cut in butter until crumbly. Stir in nuts and vanilla. Sprinkle over filling. Bake as filling directs.

Faye Weiss
Pine Bluff, Arkansas

TOASTED COCONUT TOPPING

1/2 c. moist shredded coconut, cut up

Spread coconut in shallow baking dish. Bake at 350 degrees for 10 to 15 minutes or until browned as desired.

Nancy Skinner
Jackson, Mississippi

OLD-FASHIONED COOKED MERINGUE

1 tbsp. cornstarch
4 egg whites
1 tsp. lemon juice
8 tbsp. sugar

Blend cornstarch with 2 tablespoons cold water in saucepan. Stir in 1/2 cup boiling water. Cook until thick, stirring constantly. Place saucepan in cold water to cool quickly. Beat egg whites with lemon juice until soft peaks form. Add sugar gradually, beating until stiff. Pour in cornstarch mixture; beat until well blended. Spoon onto filling, sealing to crust. Bake at 425 degrees for 5 minutes or until golden brown.

Thelma Sullivan
Sterling, Kansas

BASIC MERINGUE

4 egg whites
1/4 tsp. cream of tartar
1/2 c. sugar
3/4 tsp. vanilla extract

Beat egg whites with cream of tartar until foamy. Add sugar gradually, beating until stiff and glossy. Beat in vanilla. Spread over filling, sealing to edge. Bake at 400 degrees for 10 minutes until lightly browned.

Audry Ritter
Storm Lake, Iowa

BOILED MERINGUE TOPPING

1/2 tbsp. light corn syrup
1/2 c. sugar
2 egg whites, stiffly beaten
1/4 tsp. vanilla extract
1/4 tsp. fresh lemon juice

Combine syrup, sugar and 2 tablespoons water in saucepan. Cook to soft-ball stage or 238 degrees on candy thermometer; remove from heat. Pour over stiffly beaten egg whites in fine stream, beating constantly. Stir in vanilla and lemon juice. Spread over pie. Chill until serving time.

Bessie Morris
Fayette, Missouri

COCONUT MERINGUE

3 egg whites, beaten
1/8 tsp. salt
1/8 tsp. cream of tartar
6 tbsp. sugar
1/4 c. coconut (opt.)

Beat egg whites with salt and cream of tartar until soft peaks form. Add sugar gradually, beating until stiff. Spread over filling, sealing to edge. Sprinkle coconut over top. Bake at 400 degrees for 10 minutes until lightly browned.

Elaine Nolan
Concordia, Kansas

SIMPLE MERINGUE

4 egg whites
1/2 c. sugar

Beat egg whites until soft peaks form; add sugar gradually, beating until stiff. Spread over filling, sealing to edge. Bake at 350 degrees for 15 minutes or until lightly browned.

Loretta Wilson
Goshen, Indiana

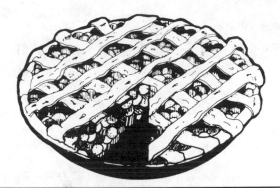

CRANBERRY SWANS, Recipe on page 100.

CLASSIC PASTRIES

BASIC CREAM PUFFS

1/2 c. butter
1/4 tsp. salt
1 c. sifted flour
4 eggs

Combine 1 cup water, butter and salt in saucepan. Bring to a full rolling boil. Reduce heat. Stir in flour quickly, mixing vigorously with wooden spoon until mixture leaves side of pan. Remove from heat. Add eggs 1 at a time, beating after each addition until smooth. Drop by large spoonfuls 3 inches apart on greased baking sheet. Bake in preheated 400-degree oven for 10 minutes. Reduce temperature to 350 degrees. Bake for 25 minutes longer or until golden and firm. Cut off tops and remove excess dough or split puffs with knife and bake for several minutes longer. Fill as desired. Yield: 1 dozen.

Petits Puffs: Drop pastry by heaping measuring teaspoonfuls onto greased baking sheet. Bake at 400 degrees for 20 minutes. Fill as desired. Yield: 8 dozen.

Eclairs: Shape pastry into 1 x 4-inch fingers on greased baking sheet. Bake as for cream puffs. Fill as desired. Yield: 1 1/4 dozen.

Glynes Vanderhoof
The Dalles, Oregon

2
EASY CREAM PUFFS

1 stick pie crust mix
2 eggs

Crumble pie crust stick into medium saucepan. Stir in 2/3 cup boiling water. Cook until pastry forms ball and leaves side of pan, stirring constantly. Cook for 1 minute over low heat, stirring constantly. Add eggs 1 at a time, beating with electric mixer at low speed for 1 minute after each addition. Drop by 3 tablespoonfuls onto greased baking sheet. Bake at 425 degrees for 15 minutes. Reduce temperature to 350 degrees. Bake until cream puffs are dry and golden brown. Remove from baking sheet; cool. Cut off tops; remove excess dough. Fill as desired.

Bernice H. Rice
Prattville, Alabama

CRANBERRY SWANS

1/2 c. shortening
1 c. flour
1/4 tsp. salt
4 eggs
1 c. heavy cream, whipped
1   6-oz. can Ocean Spray jellied cranberry
   sauce, cut into 1/2-in. cubes
1/2 tsp. rum extract
Confectioners' sugar

Heat shortening and 1 cup water in saucepan until shortening is melted. Add flour and salt all at once. Cook until dough forms ball, stirring constantly. Cool for 5 minutes. Add eggs, 1 at a time, beating until smooth and glossy. Pipe 10 "S" shapes on ungreased baking sheet. Spoon remaining batter into 10 mounds on ungreased cookie sheet. Bake mounds at 400 degrees for 30 to 35 minutes or until golden brown. Bake "S" shapes for 10 to 15 minutes. Cool. Slice off the top third of each puff. Mix whipped cream, cranberry cubes and rum flavoring in bowl. Fill puffs. Cut top slice into halves; push halves into cream to resemble wings. Push "S" shape into side of puff to resemble neck and head of swan. Sprinkle with confectioners' sugar. Serve immediately.

Photograph for this recipe on page 99.

CHERRY CREAM PUFF RING

1 recipe cream puff pastry (pg. 100)
1 c. milk
3/4 c. sour cream
1 pkg. vanilla instant pudding mix
1/4 tsp. almond extract
1 can cherry pie filling

Drop cream puff pastry by tablespoonfuls to make 8-inch circle on greased baking sheet; smooth with spatula. Bake at 400 degrees for 50 to 60 mintues or until puffed and golden. Cut off top when cool; remove soft dough in center. Combine milk, sour cream, pudding mix and flavoring in mixer bowl. Beat at low speed for 1 minute. Spoon into ring. Top with half the pie filling. Replace top of ring. Drizzle remaining pie filling over top.

Tippy Herndon
Salem, Oregon

GOLDEN RAISIN CREAM PUFFS

1/2 c. golden raisins, plumped
1 tsp. sugar
1 recipe cream puff pastry (pg. 100)
1 tbsp. butter, melted
1 1/2 tbsp. cream
1 c. confectioners' sugar
1/2 tsp. each lemon juice, vanilla extract

Stir raisins and sugar into cream puff pastry. Drop by heaping tablespoonfuls onto greased baking sheet. Bake at 375 degrees for 30 to 35 minutes or until golden and firm. Combine remaining ingredients in bowl; beat until smooth. Frost slightly cooled puffs.

Joyce Lindenberger
Inman, Kansas

CHOCOLATE CREAM PUFF MINARETS

1 recipe cream puff pastry (pg. 100)
1   8-oz. package cream cheese, softened
6 tbsp. cream
1/4 c. sugar
2 tsp. vanilla extract
1 c. semisweet chocolate chips, melted

Drop cream puff pastry 2 tablespoonfuls at a time into 8 mounds on baking sheet. Drop remaining pastry 1 teaspoonful at a time into 8 mounds on baking sheet. Bake at 400 degrees for 50 minutes. Cool. Blend cream cheese and cream in bowl. Stir in sugar and vanilla. Fold in chocolate. Chill until thick. Split large puffs in half. Fill bottom halves with cream cheese mixture. Place tops cut side up on filling. Fill with cream cheese mixture. Top with small puffs filled with remaining cream cheese mixture. Freeze until serving time. Garnish with sprinkling of confectioners' sugar.

Glennis Maltsberger
Cos Cob, Connecticut

PROFITEROLES IN CHOCOLATE SAUCE

2 c. whipping cream
6 tbsp. vanilla sugar
1 1/2 tsp. vanilla extract
8 doz. Petits Puffs (pg. 100)

2 oz. chopped unsweetened chocolate
1/2 c. sugar
6 tbsp. hot cream
Pinch of salt
1/4 c. toasted slivered almonds

Beat whipping cream with vanilla sugar and 1 teaspoon vanilla in bowl until stiff. Pipe with pastry tube into bottoms of puffs. Layer filled puffs in serving dish. Combine remaining ingredients except almonds with 1/2 teaspoon vanilla in blender container. Process until smooth, adding additional cream if necessary. Pour over puffs. Sprinkle almonds on top. Puffs may be filled with vanilla ice cream and frozen until serving time.

Brandy Elisander
Newport, Rhode Island

BUTTERSCOTCH-ALMOND CREAM PUFFS

1 recipe cream puff pastry (pg. 100)
1 c. sugar
1/2 c. flour
1/8 tsp. salt
3 c. milk, scalded
3 eggs, beaten
1 1/2 tsp. vanilla extract
1 c. whipping cream, whipped
1/2 c. slivered almonds
1 c. packed brown sugar
1/4 c. cream
2 tbsp. light corn syrup
3 tbsp. butter

Drop cream puff pastry by heaping teaspoonfuls 2 inches apart on greased baking sheet. Bake at 400 degrees for 10 minutes. Reduce temperature to 350 degrees. Bake for 25 minutes longer. Combine sugar, flour and salt in double boiler. Add hot milk gradually, stirring constantly. Add eggs. Cook for 3 minutes. Fold in vanilla, whipped cream and almonds. Spoon into puffs. Combine remaining ingredients in saucepan. Bring to a boil, stirring constantly. Reduce heat. Simmer for 3 minutes. Serve over cream puffs.

Connie Taylor
Pine Bluff, Arkansas

CREAM PUFF PYRAMID (CROQUEMBOUCHE)

1 recipe cream puff pastry (pg. 100)
1 recipe Vanilla Cream Puff Filling (pg. 103)
1 c. sugar

Drop cream puff pastry by small spoonfuls onto baking sheet. Bake at 400 degrees for 20 minutes or until puffed and golden brown. Cool. Fill pastry bag with Vanilla Cream Puff Filling. Pipe filling into puffs. Cook sugar with 2 tablespoons water in saucepan over medium heat until light golden brown; remove from heat. Dip filled cream puffs into hot syrup. Arrange in tiers of decreasing size to form pyramid on serving plate.

Cassie Swenson
Roanoke, Virginia

CREAMY APRICOT CREAM PUFFS

1 16-oz. can apricot halves, drained, pureed
2/3 c. sugar
1/4 tsp. ground cinnamon
1 c. sour cream
1 recipe cream puff pastry (pg. 100)
1 c. confectioners' sugar
2 to 3 tbsp. milk

Bring pureed apricots and sugar to a boil in medium saucepan. Simmer for 15 minutes or until very thick. Cool to room temperature. Stir in cinnamon and sour cream. Chill until serving time. Drop cream puff pastry by 1/4 cupfuls 3 inches apart on baking sheet. Bake at 400 degrees for 35 to 40 minutes or until puffed and golden brown. Cut off top 1/3 of each cooled puff. Remove excess soft dough. Spoon 1 1/2 tablespoons chilled apricot filling into each puff. Replace tops. Blend confectioners' sugar with enough milk in bowl to make glaze. Drizzle over cream puffs. Yield: 1 dozen.

Anastasia Nolan
Atlanta, Georgia

PINK CLOUD CREAM PUFFS

1 recipe cream puff pastry (pg. 100)
1/2 c. sugar
5 tbsp. flour
Dash of salt
2 c. milk
2 egg yolks, lightly beaten
1/4 c. chopped drained cherries
1 tsp. vanilla extract
Confectioners' sugar

Drop cream puff pastry by tablespoonfuls onto greased baking sheet. Bake at 400 degrees for 10 minutes. Reduce temperature to 350 degrees. Bake for 25 minutes longer. Combine sugar, flour and salt in double boiler. Add milk; mix well. Blend in egg yolks. Cook until smooth and thick, stirring constantly. Cool, stirring occasionally. Fold in cherries and vanilla. Spoon into puffs. Dust with confectioners' sugar.

Dora Bain
Sweetwater, Tennessee

CHOCOLATE-WALNUT CREAM PUFFS

2 tbsp. flour
6 tbsp. sugar
Dash of salt
3/4 c. milk
1 sq. chocolate, melted
1 tbsp. butter
1 tsp. vanilla extract
1/2 c. whipping cream, whipped
1/2 c. chopped walnuts
1 doz. cream puffs (pg. 100)
Chocolate syrup

Mix flour, sugar and salt in double boiler. Add milk and chocolate. Cook over hot water until thick, stirring constantly. Add butter and vanilla; cool. Fold in whipped cream and walnuts. Spoon into puffs. Drizzle syrup over top.

Frances Grimes
Enid, Oklahoma

CHOCOLATE-RICOTTA CREAM PUFFS

Sugar
3 tbsp. grated orange rind
1 tbsp. grated lemon rind
1 recipe cream puff pastry (pg. 100)
2 lb. ricotta cheese
1/4 c. grated sweet chocolate
4 tsp. almond extract
Milk
18 maraschino cherries

Add 1 tablespoon sugar, 1 tablespoon orange rind and lemon rind to cream puff pastry; mix well. Drop by tablespoonfuls 3 inches apart on greased baking sheet. Bake at 400 degrees for 10 minutes. Reduce temperature to 350 degrees. Bake for 30 minutes longer. Remove from oven; slit immediately to allow steam to escape. Combine cheese, chocolate, almond extract, remaining 2 tablespoons orange rind and sugar to taste in bowl. Blend in enough milk to make of custard consistency. Fill puffs with mixture; top with cherries. Yield: 1 1/2 dozen.

Priscilla Estes
Blue Hole, Nevada

CAFE AU LAIT PETITS PUFFS

1/3 c. sugar
1 c. whipping cream
2 tbsp. instant coffee powder
3 doz. Petits Puffs (pg. 100)
1 c. confectioners' sugar

Blend sugar into whipping cream gradually, beating until stiff. Dissolve coffee in 2 tablespoons boiling water. Fold half the coffee mixture into whipped cream. Spoon into puffs. Blend remaining coffee mixture with confectioners' sugar in bowl. Spread over puffs.

Drue Davidson
Emporia, Virginia

COFFEE CUSTARD CREAM PUFFS

1/4 c. flour
1 tbsp. cornstarch
3/4 c. sugar
2 c. milk, scalded
1 tbsp. butter, melted
1 egg, beaten
1/4 tsp. salt
1 1/2 tsp. instant coffee powder
1 tsp. vanilla extract
1 doz. cream puffs (pg. 100)

Mix flour, cornstarch and sugar in double boiler. Pour hot milk over flour mixture; mix well. Cook until mixture thickens, stirring constantly. Cook, covered, for 15 minutes longer. Combine butter, egg, salt and instant coffee in bowl. Stir a small amount of hot mixture into egg mixture; stir egg mixture into hot mixture.

Cook until thick and smooth, stirring constantly. Fold in vanilla. Cool to room temperature. Spoon into puffs.

Tiffany Scholes
Corpus Christy, Texas

VANILLA CREAM PUFF FILLING

3/4 c. sugar
6 tbsp. cornstarch
1/2 tsp. salt
3 c. milk, scalded
3 eggs, beaten
1 tbsp. butter
2 tsp. vanilla extract

Mix sugar, cornstarch and salt in double boiler. Stir in milk. Cook until thick, stirring constantly. Cook, covered, for 10 minutes longer. Stir a small amount of hot mixture into eggs; stir eggs into hot mixture. Cook for 5 minutes, stirring constantly. Add butter. Sprinkle a small amount of additional sugar over top to prevent skin from forming. Chill in refrigerator. Fold in vanilla.

Chocolate Cream Puff Filling: Stir 3 ounces melted chocolate into milk before adding to mixed dry ingredients.

Fluffy Cream Puff Filling: Reduce milk to 2 1/2 cups. Fold in 1 to 1 1/2 cups whipped cream with vanilla.

Lily Gross
Memphis, Tennessee

ELEGANT EGGNOG ECLAIRS

2 c. commercial eggnog
2 1/2 tbsp. cornstarch
1 tbsp. rum (opt.)
10 Eclairs (pg. 100)
Whipped cream
Chocolate sauce

Stir eggnog gradually into cornstarch in saucepan. Cook over medium heat until thickened, stirring constantly. Cool, stirring occasionally. Stir in rum. Chill in refrigerator. Spoon into Eclairs. Top with whipped cream; drizzle with chocolate sauce.

Sammie Horton
Birmingham, Michigan

ECLAIRS SUPREME

1 pkg. vanilla pudding and pie filling mix
1 1/2 c. milk
1/2 tsp. Brandy flavoring
2 c. miniature marshmallows
3 bananas, sliced
16 Eclairs (pg. 100)
1 10-oz. jar chocolate topping

Prepare pudding mix according to package directions using 1 1/2 cups milk. Stir flavoring into pudding; blend well. Chill, covered, in refrigerator. Fold in marshmallows and banana slices. Fill Eclairs with cream filling. Chill for 1 hour. Spread chocolate topping over top.

Judith Bowers
Batavia, Ohio

CHEESY APPLE DUMPLINGS

1 1/2 c. sifted flour
1 tsp. salt
2/3 c. shortening
1/2 c. oats
1/3 c. grated sharp cheese
1/2 c. packed brown sugar
1/2 tsp. cinnamon
2 tbsp. melted butter
1/4 c. raisins
6 baking apples, peeled, cored

Sift flour and salt together into bowl. Cut in shortening until crumbly. Add oats and cheese; mix lightly. Add 6 to 8 tablespoons water, a small amount at a time, mixing until dough may be shaped into ball. Roll on floured surface into 14 x 21-inch rectangle. Cut into 6 squares. Mix brown sugar, cinnamon, butter and raisins in bowl. Place apples on dough squares. Fill centers of apples with raisin mixture. Bring corners of dough over apples; pinch edges together to seal. Prick with fork; place in shallow baking pan. Bake at 400 degrees for 40 minutes or until apples are tender.

Bernadette Portman
Big Clifty, Kentucky

BANANA DUMPLINGS WITH LEMON SAUCE

1 recipe 2-crust pie pastry
4 bananas, halved crosswise
Sugar
Grated lemon rind
1/2 tbsp. cornstarch
Pinch of salt
1/4 c. lemon juice
1/2 tsp. nutmeg
3 tbsp. butter

Roll pastry into 8 circles. Place banana half on each circle. Sprinkle with sugar and rind. Fold pastry to enclose filling; seal edges. Place on baking sheet. Pinch with fork; sprinkle with additional sugar. Bake at 425 degrees for 45 minutes. Combine 3/4 cup sugar, cornstarch and salt in double boiler. Add 1 1/2 cups boiling water; mix well. Cook until clear and thick, stirring constantly. Add remaining ingredients, stirring until butter melts. Serve over Banana Dumplings.

Glenda Charles
Wilmington, Delaware

EASY PEACH DUMPLINGS

1 1/2 c. sugar
3 tbsp. butter
1 3/4 tsp. cinnamon
6 peaches, peeled, halved
1 recipe pie pastry

Combine 1 cup sugar, 2 cups water, butter and 1/4 teaspoon cinnamon in saucepan. Cook for 3 minutes. Mix remaining 1/2 cup sugar and 1 1/2 teaspoons cinnamon. Sprinkle into centers of peach halves. Place peach halves together. Roll pastry on floured surface. Cut into 6 squares. Place peaches on pastry. Bring corners together; seal edges. Place in baking dish. Pour cooked mixture over dumplings. Bake at 400 degrees for 40 minutes, basting frequently.

Harriette McGhee
St. Louis, Missouri

FRESH PEAR DUMPLINGS

1 c. sugar
1/8 tsp. each cinnamon, nutmeg
2 drops of red food coloring
2 tbsp. butter
2 c. flour
2 tsp. baking powder
1 tsp. salt
2/3 c. shortening

1/2 c. milk
6 pears, peeled, cored

Mix 1 cup water, sugar, cinnamon, nutmeg and food coloring in saucepan. Bring to a boil. Add butter. Sift flour, baking powder and salt together into a bowl and cut in shortening. Add milk and mix well. Roll out; cut into 6 squares. Wrap square of pastry around each pear. Place in baking pan. Pour syrup over dumplings. Bake at 375 degrees for about 45 minutes.

Francine Bartley
Charleston, West Virginia

APPLE-RAISIN PIE FRY

2 1/2 c. canned apple slices, drained,
   chopped
3/4 c. packed light brown sugar
1 tsp. cinnamon
1/2 tsp. nutmeg
1/4 tsp. allspice
1/4 c. seedless raisins
Flour
2 tbsp. sugar
1/2 tsp. salt
2/3 c. shortening
Oil for deep frying
Confectioners' sugar

Combine first 6 ingredients and 1 tablespoon flour in bowl; mix well. Sift 2 cups sifted flour, sugar and salt into bowl. Cut in shortening until crumbly. Stir in 1/4 cup water. Roll 1/8-inch thick on floured surface. Cut into 5-inch circles. Spoon apple mixture onto circles. Moisten edges with water. Fold over to enclose filling; seal edges with fork. Deep-fry in 350-degree oil for 4 minutes. Drain on paper towels. Dust with confectioners' sugar. Yield: 1 1/2 dozen.

Georgette Clark
Clayton, Missouri

DOUBLE CHEESE-APPLE FRIED PIES

3 c. chopped peeled apples
2 tbsp. butter
4 tsp. lemon juice
1 c. grated Cheddar cheese
1/4 to 1/3 c. sugar
1 tsp. cinnamon

1/2 tsp. nutmeg
1 recipe 2-crust cheese pastry
1/4 c. (or more) shortening

Simmer apples in 1/3 cup hot water in covered saucepan for 5 to 10 minutes or until tender-crisp. Drain well. Add butter and lemon juice. Combine cheese, sugar, cinnamon and nutmeg in bowl; mix well. Add to apples. Set aside. Roll pastry on floured surface. Cut into 6-inch circles. Spoon 2 tablespoons apple mixture onto each circle. Moisten edges with water. Fold over; seal edges with fork. Fry in hot shortening in skillet until golden brown on both sides, adding additional shortening if necessary. Top with ice cream, whipped cream, sharp cheese or confectioners' sugar.

Roberta Howard
Charlottesville, Virginia

PEACHY FRIED PIES

1 1/2 c. (scant) shortening
3 c. flour
1 egg
1 tbsp. vinegar
1 tbsp. sugar
1 1/2 tbsp. cornstarch
1 1/4 c. peach syrup
1 tbsp. lemon juice
1 tbsp. butter
Pinch of salt
1/4 tsp. almond extract
1 20-oz. can sliced peaches, drained
Oil for deep frying

Cut shortening into flour in bowl until crumbly. Beat egg, 5 tablespoons ice water and vinegar together until well mixed. Add to shortening mixture; mix well. Chill for 30 minutes. Combine sugar and cornstarch in saucepan. Add peach syrup gradually, stirring to mix well. Cook over low heat until thick, stirring constantly. Remove from heat. Add lemon juice, butter, salt and almond extract. Stir until butter is melted. Fold in peaches; cool. Roll pastry on floured surface. Cut into circles. Place a small amount of peach filling on each circle. Fold over; seal edges with fork. Deep-fry in 1/2-inch 370-degree oil for 10 minutes or until brown, turning once. Drain on paper towel.

Joan A. Bradshaw
San Antonio, Texas

FRIED PINEAPPLE PIES

1 recipe pie pastry
1 can pineapple pie filling
Oil for deep frying

Roll pastry on floured surface. Cut into circles. Cover half of each circle with pie filling. Fold over; seal edges. Fry in deep hot oil until brown.

Amanda Hunt
Leesburg, Florida

FRIED RAISIN PIES

1 lb. raisins
1/2 orange, thinly sliced
1/4 lemon, thinly sliced
1/2 c. butter
1 c. sugar
1 recipe pie pastry
Oil for deep frying

Place raisins, orange and lemon in saucepan with water to cover. Cook for 15 minutes; remove from heat. Add butter and sugar; mix well. Chill in refrigerator. Roll pastry on floured surface; cut into 4-inch circles. Place 2 tablespoons raisin mixture on each circle. Fold over; press edges together. Fry in deep hot oil until brown.

Jimmy D. Luttrell
Fort Worth, Texas

RAISIN-APPLE FRITTERS WITH RAISIN LEMON SAUCE

1 c. sifted flour
1/2 tsp. salt
1 tbsp. sugar
1 egg, beaten
1 c. milk
1 tbsp. melted butter
1/2 c. California raisins, chopped
4 apples, peeled, cored, sliced in rounds
Oil for frying
Raisin Lemon Sauce

Sift flour, salt and sugar into bowl. Beat egg with milk and butter. Add to dry ingredients all at once; stir until smooth. Fold in raisins. Dip apple slices into batter. Deep-fry at 370 degrees until golden brown. Serve hot with Raisin Lemon Sauce.

RAISIN-APPLE FRITTERS WITH
RAISIN LEMON SAUCE

Raisin Lemon Sauce

1/2 c. sugar
1 tbsp. cornstarch
1/8 tsp. salt
1/8 tsp. nutmeg
2 tbsp. butter
1/2 c. California raisins
1/8 tsp. grated lemon rind
2 tbsp. lemon juice

Combine sugar, cornstarch, salt, nutmeg and 1 cup water in saucepan. Cook until thick and clear, stirring constantly. Remove from heat; add remaining ingredients. Yield: 1 1/2 cups sauce.

Photograph for this recipe above.

BASIC PUFF PASTRY

3 c. flour
1 c. cake flour
2 tsp. salt
1 lb. unsalted butter

Sift flours and salt into bowl. Add 1/4 of the butter cut into small pieces. Rub butter into flour with fingertips. Add 10 to 12 tablespoons cold water, several tablespoonfuls at a time, until dough just clings together. Shape into ball.

Chill dough wrapped in plastic. Spread remaining butter into 6-inch square between two sheets of waxed paper. Chill for 30 minutes. Roll dough on lightly floured board into 12-inch square. Place chilled butter diagonally in center of dough; fold corners of dough over butter to meet in center. Roll into 12 x 18-inch rectangle. Fold dough into thirds; turn 90 degrees. Roll into rectangle; fold into thirds. Chill, wrapped, for 1 hour or longer. Repeat rolling and turning. Chill for 2 hours. Repeat. Chill for 4 hours. Dough may be stored, tightly wrapped, in refrigerator for 2 or 3 days or frozen for 2 to 3 months. Thaw overnight in refrigerator.

Patty Shells: Roll chilled dough into 7 x 16-inch rectangle. Cut into circles with hot 3 1/4-inch cutter. Cut smaller circles 2/3 through dough with 2 1/2-inch cutter. Place on baking sheet. Chill in refrigerator. Bake in preheated 450-degree oven for 10 minutes. Reduce temperature to 350 degrees. Bake for 20 minutes longer or until browned. Remove and reserve centers. Fill as desired. Place centers on top.

Vol-Au-Vent: Roll chilled dough into 9 x 17-inch rectangle. Cut into two 8-inch circles. Place 1 circle on baking sheet. Cut 5-inch circle from center of remaining circle. Place 8-inch ring on 8-inch circle. Place 5-inch circle on baking sheet. Chill in refrigerator. Bake in preheated 450-degree oven for 10 minutes. Reduce temperature to 350 degrees. Bake for 20 minutes longer or until browned. Fill shell as desired. Top with smaller circle.

Puff pastry may also be used for tarts, turnovers, pie shells and dumplings. Bake filled dough at 450 degrees for 15 minutes. Reduce temperature to 350 degrees. Bake until deep golden brown.

Mary Cummings
Larchmont, New York

CREAM HORNS

1 recipe puff pastry (pg. 106)
Apricot jam
1/2 pt. whipping cream
2 tbsp. sugar
1/2 c. chopped pistachio nuts

Roll chilled dough into 4 x 24-inch rectangle. Cut into 8 long strips. Wrap each strip around cream horn mold, starting from small end and overlapping dough on turns. Place on baking sheet lined with baking parchment. Chill for 1 hour. Bake at 425 degrees for 20 minutes or until golden. Remove molds while warm. Dry in 180-degree oven for several minutes if necessary. Brush insides with jam. Fill with whipping cream whipped with sugar. Sprinkle nuts over whipped cream.

Francie Brookshire
Canton, Ohio

PALM LEAVES (PALMIERS GLACES)

1 recipe puff pastry (pg. 106)
Sugar

Roll chilled dough into rectangle. Sprinkle heavily with sugar. Roll lightly to press sugar into dough. Fold short edges to center. Sprinkle with sugar; roll lightly. Bring folded edges to center. Sprinkle with sugar; roll lightly. Bring folded edges together to fold in half. Chill, wrapped, for 1 hour. Cut into 3/8-inch slices. Place 2 inches apart on baking sheet lined with baking parchment. Pinch ends outward from center into slightly belled shape. Bake at 425 degrees for 15 minutes. Turn pastries over. Bake for 10 minutes longer or until brown.

Noel Blaisdell
Little Rock, Arkansas

STRAWBERRY PASTRY CAKE

1 recipe puff pastry (pg. 106)
4 c. fresh strawberries, sweetened
1 jar raspberry preserves
1 tbsp. lemon juice

Roll chilled dough into 10 x 15-inch rectangle. Place on baking sheet lined with baking parchment. Fold long edges toward center. Cut narrow strip from each folded edge. Chill for 1 hour. Prick with fork. Bake at 375 degrees for 25 minutes or until browned. Place on serving plate. Top with strawberries. Drizzle with mixture of warmed preserves and lemon juice.

Faith Whelan
Erie, Pennsylvania

GREEK BAKLAVA

8 c. chopped walnuts
1 tsp. cinnamon
1/4 tsp. nutmeg
7 1/4 c. sugar
2 lb. phyllo
1 1/2 lb. butter, melted
Juice of 1/2 lemon
1 stick cinnamon

Combine walnuts, cinnamon, nutmeg and 1/4 cup sugar in bowl; mix well. Cover phyllo with damp towel. Brush each sheet phyllo with melted butter. Layer 6 sheets into buttered 12 x 17-inch baking pan. Add layer of walnut mixture. Repeat layers, ending with 9 sheets buttered phyllo. Cut through phyllo with sharp knife to make 1 1/2 to 2-inch diamonds or squares. Bake in preheated 325-degree oven for 1 hour and 30 minutes to 2 hours. Combine 7 cups sugar, 5 cups water, lemon juice and cinnamon stick in saucepan. Boil for about 30 minutes or until syrupy. Pour over warm Baklava.

Ethel Patrick
Green Falls, Montana

HORSESHOE PASTRIES (BOORMA)

4 phyllo sheets
1/2 c. melted butter
1 1/2 c. chopped pecans
1/4 c. sugar
Pinch each of nutmeg, cinnamon, cloves
1/2 c. honey

Cut phyllo into eight 9 x 18-inch rectangles. Brush each with butter. Sprinkle with mixture of pecans, sugar and spices. Roll as for jelly roll. Bend into horseshoe shape. Arrange on baking sheet. Brush with butter. Bake in preheated 350-degree oven for 12 minutes or until golden. Drizzle with honey.

Sierra Smith
Lansing, Michigan

NUT PASTRIES (FLOGHERES)

1 c. ground almonds
1/2 c. cracker meal
1 egg
5 phyllo sheets
1 c. melted butter

1 c. sugar
1/2 tsp. cinnamon

Combine first 3 ingredients in bowl; mix well. Cut phyllo sheets into 4 strips; cover with damp cloth. Brush strips 1 at a time with butter. Place 1 teaspoon almond mixture on 1 end. Roll from short side as for jelly roll. Place in greased baking pan. Drizzle with remaining butter. Bake at 350 degrees for 25 minutes or until golden. Combine sugar, cinnamon and 1/2 cup water in saucepan. Boil until slightly thickened. Pour over hot pastries.

Jana Ballard
Albany, New York

BASIC STRUDEL DOUGH

4 c. flour
2 tsp. salt
2 eggs, lightly beaten
1/2 c. melted unsalted butter
1 tsp. lemon juice (opt.)

Sift flour and salt into large bowl. Make well in center. Mix eggs, 2 1/2 cups water, half the butter and lemon juice in bowl. Pour into well in flour. Stir until smooth. Knead on floured surface for 10 minutes or until smooth, shiny and blistered on surface. Brush generously with melted butter. Place in bowl. Let rest, covered, for 30 minutes. Cover large table completely with floured cloth. Place dough in center of cloth. Roll as thin as possible. Spread a small amount of melted butter over dough. Stretch with hands, working carefully around table to avoid tearing the dough until very thin and almost transparent. Brush dough with butter as necessary. Cut off any thick edges. Let dough rest for about 15 minutes before continuing to complete strudel recipe.

Tammy Schrunk
Rockford, Illinois

HOLIDAY APPLE STRUDEL

8 c. chopped peeled tart apples
1/2 recipe strudel dough (pg. 108)
1/2 c. chopped blanched almonds
1 1/2 c. seedless raisins
1 tbsp. grated lemon rind
1 c. sugar

1/3 c. dry bread crumbs
3 tbsp. melted butter

Arrange apples over surface of stretched strudel dough. Sprinkle with almonds, raisins and mixture of rind, sugar, crumbs and butter. Fold sides in. Roll gently as for jelly roll. Place on baking sheet. Brush with additional melted butter. Bake at 400 degrees for about 20 minutes. Reduce temperature to 350 degrees. Bake for about 10 minutes longer or until golden brown.

Dominque Armenti
Raleigh, North Carolina

CHEESE STRUDEL

1/4 c. butter, softened
2 c. cottage cheese
4 egg yolks
2 eggs
1/3 c. sugar
1 tsp. vanilla extract
1/2 recipe strudel dough (pg. 108)
Melted butter

Combine softened butter, cottage cheese, egg yolks, 1 egg, sugar and vanilla in bowl; mix well. Brush stretched dough with remaining beaten egg. Spoon filling down length of dough 3 inches from edge. Fold in ends. Roll gently as for jelly roll. Place on baking sheet. Brush with melted butter. Bake at 400 degrees for about 20 minutes. Reduce temperature to 350 degrees. Bake for about 10 minutes longer or until golden brown.

Queenie Rasmussan
Syracuse, New York

CHOCOLATE STRUDEL

6 eggs, separated
6 tbsp. sugar
4 oz. semisweet chocolate, grated
1 c. finely ground walnuts
1 tsp. vanilla extract
1/2 recipe strudel dough (pg. 108)
1/2 c. melted butter
1/2 c. fine bread crumbs

Beat egg yolks with sugar in bowl until thick. Add chocolate, walnuts and vanilla. Fold in stiffly beaten egg whites. Brush stretched strudel dough with butter; sprinkle with crumbs.

Spread chocolate filling over 1/3 of the dough 3 inches in from edge. Fold ends over. Roll as for jelly roll. Place on baking sheet. Bake at 350 degrees for 45 minutes or until golden, brushing with butter several times.

Edwina Keithley
Miami, Florida

PINEAPPLE STRUDEL

1/2 recipe strudel dough (pg. 108)
1 c. melted butter
1/2 c. dry bread crumbs
1 1/2 c. sugar
1 tsp. cinnamon
4 c. chopped fresh pineapple
1/2 c. chopped maraschino cherries
1 c. seedless raisins
1 c. ground walnuts

Brush stretched strudel dough with butter. Sprinkle with crumbs, sugar and cinnamon. Spread pineapple, cherries, raisins and walnuts over 3/4 of the dough. Drizzle with butter. Fold ends in. Roll as for jelly roll. Place on baking sheet. Brush with butter. Bake at 375 degrees for 45 minutes or until brown, brushing frequently with butter.

Angelina Fierro
San Diego, California

APPLE TART

1 3/4 c. flour
Pinch of salt
1 stick butter, softened
1 3/4 lb. apples, peeled, sliced
1/4 c. sugar
Black currant jelly, melted

Combine flour and salt in bowl. Cut in butter until crumbly. Add 3 tablespoons water; mix well. Let stand in lightly floured cloth for 1 hour. Roll until thin on floured surface. Line buttered and floured 10-inch pie pan with dough. Cut to fit; prick bottom with fork. Arrange apple slices slightly overlapping on dough. Sprinkle with sugar. Bake at 400 degrees for 35 to 40 minutes or until brown. Spoon jelly over hot apples.

Patricia A. Smith
Smithfield, Virginia

EASY FRESH FRUIT TART

1 8-oz. roll refrigerator sugar cookies,
   sliced 1/8 in. thick
1 8-oz. package cream cheese, softened
1/3 c. sugar
1/2 tsp. vanilla extract
Grapes, strawberries, banana slices, orange
   slices, apple wedges, blueberries,
   kiwi slices and fresh pineapple chunks
1/2 c. orange marmalade

Line 14-inch pizza pan with cookie slices, overlapping slightly. Bake at 375 degrees for 12 minutes or until golden brown. Blend cream cheese, sugar and vanilla in bowl. Spread over cooled crust. Arrange fruit over cream cheese layer. Blend marmalade with 2 tablespoons water in bowl. Drizzle over fruit. Chill in refrigerator. Cut into wedges to serve.

Debbie Hobaugh
Braman, Oklahoma

GLACE FRUIT TART

1/2 c. butter, softened
1/2 c. sugar
1 egg white
1 c. sifted flour
3/4 c. ground blanched almonds
1/2 tsp. almond extract
1 tbsp. cornstarch
1 c. milk
2 egg yolks, beaten
3/4 tsp. vanilla extract
2 c. strawberries
1 c. fresh raspberries
1 c. fresh blueberries
1 c. fresh Royal Anne cherries
1 3-oz. package lemon gelatin

Combine butter and 1/4 cup sugar in medium bowl. Beat in egg white. Add flour, almonds and almond extract; mix well. Press onto bottom and side of 10-inch tart pan. Bake at 375 degrees until golden brown. Cool. Combine remaining 1/4 cup sugar, cornstarch and milk in small saucepan. Bring to a boil over medium heat, stirring constantly. Remove from heat. Beat in egg yolks quickly; stir in vanilla. Cool. Chill, covered, overnight. Spoon into tart shell. Arrange fruit over filling. Chill in refrigerator.

Dissolve gelatin in 1 cup boiling water. Stir in 1/2 cup ice water. Chill until thick. Spoon over fruit. Chill until set. Garnish with lemon leaves.

Beverly Blair
Salem, Virginia

GERMAN PLUM TART

2 3/4 c. flour
4 1/2 tsp. baking powder
1 c. sugar
1/2 tsp. salt
4 tbsp. margarine
1 egg, beaten
6 tbsp. milk
Blue plums, halved
2 tbsp. butter
Cream

Sift 2 cups flour, 4 teaspoons baking powder, 1/4 cup sugar and salt together into bowl. Cut in margarine until crumbly. Combine egg and milk. Add to dry ingredients; mix well. Pat onto cookie sheet, crimping to make rim. Arrange plums over top. Combine remaining 3/4 cup flour, 3/4 cup sugar and 1/2 teaspoon baking powder in bowl; mix well. Cut in butter and enough cream to make coarse crumbs. Spread over plums. Bake at 375 degrees for 30 minutes.

Elsie White
Seattle, Washington

CHESS TARTLETS

1 1/2 sticks butter, softened
2 c. sugar
6 eggs
1 tbsp. cream
2 tbsp. cornmeal
1 tsp. vanilla extract
1 tbsp. vinegar
Dash of salt
12 unbaked 3-in. tart shells

Cream butter and sugar in bowl. Add eggs 1 at a time, beating well after each addition. Add next 5 ingredients; mix well. Spoon into tart shells. Bake at 350 degrees until filling tests done.

Melinda Pitts
Prescott, Arizona

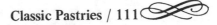

APRICOT CREAM TARTLETS

    2 16-oz. cans apricot halves, drained
    1 sm. package vanilla pudding and pie filling
       mix
    1 c. light cream
    3/4 tsp. grated lemon rind
    1/2 c. sugar
    10 baked 3-in. tart shells
    1/2 c. apricot preserves, melted, strained
    1/2 c. heavy cream, whipped, sweetened

Puree half the apricots in blender. Blend apricot puree, pudding mix, cream, lemon rind and sugar in medium saucepan. Bring to a boil, stirring constantly. Remove from heat. Spoon into tart shells. Chill until serving time. Arrange remaining apricot halves on top. Brush with preserves. Top with whipped cream. Yield: 10 tarts.

Renata Walsh
Torrance, Wyoming

LEMON-CREAM CHEESE TARTLETS

    3 eggs
    3/4 c. sugar
    2 tsp. grated lemon rind
    1/2 c. lemon juice
    1 8-oz. package cream cheese, softened,
       chopped
    10 baked 3-in. tart shells

Beat eggs in double boiler until pale and frothy. Beat in sugar gradually until thick. Stir in lemon rind and juice. Cook over simmering water for 5 minutes or until thickened, stirring constantly. Remove from heat. Add cream cheese gradually, beating constantly until well blended. Cool. Spoon into tart shells. Refrigerate, loosely covered, until serving time.

Jean Dickson
Jamestown, North Dakota

PEACH TARTLETS

    1/2 c. butter, softened
    1/4 tsp. salt
    1 egg white
    Flour
    Sugar
    Dash of salt

    2 egg yolks
    1/4 c. milk
    1/2 c. whipping cream, whipped
    1/2 tsp. vanilla extract
    Peach slices
    1/2 c. peach preserves, melted, strained

Combine first 3 ingredients, 1 1/2 cups sifted flour and 1/4 cup sugar in bowl; mix well. Press into 2-inch tart pans. Chill for 30 minutes. Bake at 375 degrees for 12 minutes. Cool in pans for several minutes before removing. Mix 2 tablespoons sugar and 2 tablespoons flour with salt in small saucepan. Stir in combined egg yolks and milk. Cook over medium heat until mixture boils and thickens, whisking constantly. Cool in bowl of ice water for 8 to 10 minutes, stirring occasionally. Fold in whipped cream and vanilla. Chill for 30 minutes. Spoon into tart shells. Top with peaches. Glaze with preserves. Chill until serving time.

Regina Willson
Corrigan

RASPBERRY TARTLETS

    1 c. shortening
    1 1/4 c. sugar
    1 egg, beaten
    1/2 tsp. salt
    1 tsp. vanilla extract
    3 c. flour
    2 cans lemon pudding
    2 c. sour cream
    2 10-oz. packages frozen raspberries, thawed
    2 tbsp. cornstarch

Cream shortening and 1 cup sugar in bowl. Add egg, salt, vanilla and flour; mix well. Press dough into 20 muffin cups. Bake at 350 degrees for 10 minutes or until golden. Cool. Blend pudding and sour cream in bowl. Chill in refrigerator. Drain raspberries well; reserve syrup. Combine remaining 1/4 cup sugar and cornstarch in small saucepan. Stir in reserved syrup gradually. Cook until mixture thickens, stirring constantly. Chill slightly. Fill tart shells with lemon mixture. Top with raspberries. Spoon 1 tablespoon raspberry glaze over each tart. Chill for 1 hour.

Margo Van Dan
Woodstock, Illinois

MAPLE WALNUT TARTLETS

1/2 c. butter
3/4 c. packed light brown sugar
1/2 c. maple syrup
3 eggs
1/4 c. heavy cream
1 1/4 c. chopped walnuts
1/2 tsp. vanilla extract
8 unbaked 3-in. tart shells
Whipped cream
8 walnut halves

Combine first 3 ingredients in saucepan. Heat to boiling point. Beat eggs lightly in large bowl. Stir in cream, chopped walnuts and vanilla. Mix in hot mixture gradually. Pour into tart shells. Bake at 375 degrees for 20 minutes or until custard tests done. Garnish cooled tarts with whipped cream. Top with walnut halves.

Susan Prinsen
Atlanta, Georgia

PINEAPPLE TARTLETS

1 pkg. lemon gelatin
2 c. miniature marshmallows
1 can crushed pineapple
1/2 c. sugar
1 c. chopped walnuts
1 c. whipping cream, whipped
6 baked 3-in. tart shells

Dissolve gelatin in 1 1/2 cups hot water. Add marshmallows; stir to dissolve. Stir next 3 ingredients into cooled marshmallow mixture; mix until sugar dissolves. Chill until thick. Fold in whipped cream. Pour into tart shells. Chill until firm.

Dorothy Moore
Sand Springs, Oklahoma

PRALINE CRESCENT TARTLETS

1/3 c. margarine, melted
1/2 c. packed brown sugar
1 tbsp. sour cream
1 c. crisp rice cereal
1/2 c. chopped pecans
1/2 c. coconut
1   8-oz. can refrigerator crescent dinner rolls
1   3-oz. package cream cheese, softened
2 tbsp. confectioners' sugar

Blend margarine and brown sugar in saucepan. Cook for 2 minutes, stirring occasionally. Remove from heat. Stir in sour cream, cereal, pecans and coconut until evenly coated. Separate roll dough into triangles. Press each triangle into muffin cup, covering bottom and side. Blend cream cheese with confectioners' sugar in bowl. Place rounded teaspoonful in each cup, spreading to cover bottom. Top with heaping tablespoonful cereal mixture. Bake at 375 degrees for 11 to 16 minutes or until deep golden brown. Top with whipped cream.

Carrie Smith
Bakersville, Ohio

EASY CHERRY TASSIES

Vanilla wafer crumbs
2   8-oz. packages cream cheese, softened
2 eggs
1 c. sugar
1 tsp. vanilla extract
1 can cherry pie filling

Spread crumbs in bottom of paper-lined miniature muffin cups. Beat remaining ingredients except pie filling in bowl until smooth. Spoon over crumbs. Bake at 350 degrees for 10 minutes. Top with pie filling when cool.

Linda Cherry
Griggsville, Illinois

PECAN TASSIES

2   3-oz. packages cream cheese, softened
2 sticks margarine, softened
2 c. flour
2 eggs, beaten
1 1/2 c. packed brown sugar
2 tbsp. melted margarine
2 tsp. vanilla extract
Pinch of salt
1 1/2 c. chopped pecans

Combine cream cheese, margarine and flour in bowl; mix well. Chill in refrigerator. Shape into walnut-sized balls. Press over bottoms and halfway up side of miniature muffin cups. Mix remaining 6 ingredients in order listed in bowl. Spoon into prepared muffin cups. Bake at 350 degrees for 25 minutes. Cool in pan.

Ginger Fink
Demmitt, Texas

WALNUT TASSIES

1/2 lb. margarine, softened
1 8-oz. package cream cheese, softened
2 1/2 c. flour
1 c. chopped walnuts
4 eggs
1 box brown sugar
2 tbsp. melted margarine
1/2 tsp. vanilla extract

Combine first 3 ingredients in bowl; mix well. Chill for 1 hour. Shape into balls. Press into miniature tart pans. Place a small amount of chopped walnuts in each shell. Beat eggs into brown sugar in bowl 1 at a time. Add margarine and vanilla; mix well. Spoon into tart shells. Bake at 350 degrees for 15 to 20 minutes or until set.

Shelby Francis
Claremont, New Hampshire

EASY PEANUT BUTTER TASSIES

1/2 c. margarine, softened
1/2 c. peanut butter
1/2 c. sugar
1/2 c. packed brown sugar
1 egg
1/2 tsp. vanilla extract
1 1/4 c. flour
3/4 tsp. soda
1/2 tsp. salt
1 10-oz. box miniature peanut butter cups

Cream margarine, peanut butter and sugars in bowl. Beat in egg and vanilla. Blend in dry ingredients. Roll into small balls. Press into 1 1/2-inch fluted tart cups. Bake at 375 degrees for 8 to 10 minutes or until light brown. Press 1 peanut butter cup into each hot shell. Cool in pan for 10 minutes. Yield: 40 servings.

Shari Godwin
DeGraff, Ohio

LEMON CURD TASSIES

2 tbsp. butter, melted
1 1/2 c. sugar
Grated rind of 3 lemons
9 tbsp. lemon juice
3 eggs, well beaten
24 baked miniature tart shells

Combine first 5 ingredients in saucepan in order listed, mixing well after each addition. Cook over medium heat until thick, stirring constantly. Set aside to cool. Spoon 1 tablespoon lemon filling into each tart shell. Top with unsweetened whipped cream.

Eva Cantor
Hartfield, Connecticut

APPLE CHEESEOVERS

2 c. canned applesauce
1 tsp. cinnamon
1 tsp. cornstarch
1 recipe cream cheese pie pastry
3/4 c. shredded sharp cheese
Sugar

Mix applesauce, cinnamon and cornstarch blended with 1 tablespoon cold water in saucepan. Cook over moderate heat for 15 minutes or until nearly dry, stirring constantly. Roll out pastry; cut into 3-inch rounds. Place scant tablespoon applesauce mixture and 1 teaspoon cheese on half of each round. Moisten edges. Fold over; seal and cut vents. Place on baking sheet. Bake at 425 degrees for 15 minutes or until browned. Sprinkle tops lightly with sugar. Serve hot. Yield: 3 dozen.

Photograph for this recipe below.

APPLE CHEESEOVERS

APPLE DELIGHTS

1 c. shortening
1 tsp. salt
1 12-oz. carton cottage cheese
2 c. flour
6 apples, peeled, sliced
Cinnamon sugar
Confectioners' sugar icing

Combine first 4 ingredients in bowl. Mix until mixture forms ball. Chill for 30 minutes. Roll on floured surface. Cut into 6 squares. Place apples on each square. Sprinkle with cinnamon sugar. Fold dough to enclose filling; seal edges. Place on greased baking sheet. Bake for 30 minutes at 400 degrees. Frost with confectioners' sugar icing.

Marianne Hartford
Meridian, Mississippi

BLUEBERRY TURNOVERS

1 1/2 c. fresh blueberries
2 tbsp. flour
1 tsp. lemon juice
1/2 c. confectioners' sugar
1 recipe pie pastry
5 tsp. butter
1 egg white, slightly beaten

Spread blueberries on large flat plate. Sprinkle with flour; roll berries by tipping plate until all flour is absorbed. Sprinkle with lemon juice and confectioners' sugar. Roll berries again. Roll pastry 1/8 inch thick on lightly floured surface. Cut into 4-inch squares. Spread as many berries as half the square will hold. Dot with 1/2 teaspoon butter. Fold pastry to form triangle; seal edges. Brush with egg white. Bake at 400 degrees for 10 to 15 minutes or until lightly browned. Serve hot. Yield: 10 turnovers.

Photograph for this recipe on this page.

CHERRY TURNOVERS

1 3-oz. package cream cheese, softened
Sugar
1 tbsp. fresh lemon juice
2 tsp. almond extract
1 3/4 c. drained tart cherries
1/4 c. cherry juice

2 tbsp. cornstarch
4 drops of red food coloring
3 c. flour
1 tsp. salt
1 1/4 c. shortening
1 egg
1 tbsp. vinegar
1 egg white, beaten

Combine cream cheese, 3 tablespoons sugar and lemon juice in bowl; mix well. Chill cheese filling in refrigerator. Combine 3/4 cup sugar, 1/2 teaspoon almond extract and next 4 ingredients in saucepan. Cook over medium heat until thick, stirring constantly. Set cherry filling aside to cool. Mix flour and salt in bowl. Cut in shortening until crumbly. Add remaining 1 1/2 teaspoons almond extract, 4 tablespoons cold water, beaten egg and vinegar; mix well. Roll on floured surface. Cut into 6-inch circles. Place 1 teaspoon cheese filling in center of each circle; top with 1 tablespoon cherry filling. Fold over. Moisten edges with cold water; press together with fork. Brush with egg white. Place on baking sheet. Bake at 425 degrees for 20 to 25 minutes. Yield: 1 dozen.

Cecilia Holcomb
Garber, Oklahoma

BLUEBERRY TURNOVERS

APRICOT ANGELS

2 c. butter
2 8-oz. packages cream cheese, softened
4 c. flour
2 c. sugar
4 c. apricot preserves
2 eggs, beaten

Combine butter, cream cheese and flour in bowl; mix well. Shape into ball. Refrigerate for 24 hours. Roll out thin on pastry cloth. Cut into 5-inch squares. Sprinkle with sugar. Place preserves in center of each square. Moisten edges with eggs. Fold over; seal edges. Place on baking sheet; brush tops lightly with eggs. Bake at 425 degrees for 15 to 20 minutes or until brown.

Ruby Gentry
Pleasant Hill, California

SWEET POTATO TURNOVERS

1 3-oz. package cream cheese, softened
1/4 lb. butter, softened
1 c. sifted flour
1/2 c. mashed cooked sweet potatoes
1/4 c. drained crushed pineapple
1/4 c. sugar
1/4 tsp. salt
1/4 c. flaked coconut

Combine first 3 ingredients in bowl with pastry blender. Roll on floured surface. Cut into 3-inch circles. Combine sweet potatoes and remaining ingredients in bowl; mix well. Place 1 heaping teaspoon filling on one side of each pastry circle. Fold pastry over filling; press edges together. Place on lightly greased baking sheet. Bake at 375 degrees for 8 to 12 minutes or until lightly browned.

Virginia S. McEwen
Rockford, Alabama

ALMOND PUFF

Margarine
2 c. flour
2 1/2 tsp. almond extract
3 eggs
1 1/2 c. confectioners' sugar

Cut 1/2 cup margarine into 1 cup flour in bowl until crumbly. Sprinkle 2 tablespoons water over mixture; mix well. Pat into two 3 x 12-inch strips on baking sheet. Combine 1/2 cup margarine with 1 cup water in saucepan. Bring to a boil; remove from heat. Stir in 1 teaspoon flavoring and 1 cup flour. Cook over low heat until mixture forms ball, stirring constantly. Remove from heat. Beat in eggs. Spread over strips. Bake at 350 degrees for 1 hour. Cool. Blend confectioners' sugar with 2 tablespoons softened margarine, 1 1/2 teaspoons flavoring and 2 tablespoons warm water in small bowl. Spread over cooled strips. Garnish with almonds. Yield: 20 servings.

Heather Lowe
Salt Lake City, Utah

DATE-STUFFED GREEK PASTRIES

Sugar
1 stick cinnamon
1/2 lb. unsalted butter, softened
2 egg yolks
1 c. oil
1 c. orange juice
1 oz. rum
1/4 tsp. salt
2 tsp. baking powder
1/3 tsp. soda
7 1/2 c. sifted flour
Dates, pitted
Walnut halves
1 1/2 c. ground walnuts
1/2 tsp. cinnamon

Combine 4 cups sugar, cinnamon stick and 3 cups water in saucepan. Boil for 10 minutes. Set aside to cool. Cream butter and 1 cup sugar in bowl. Add next 8 ingredients; mix well. Stuff dates with walnut halves. Roll dough 1/4 inch thick on floured surface. Cut into rectangles. Cover each date with dough, sealing edges. Place on baking sheet. Bake at 375 degrees for 45 minutes or until golden brown. Combine ground walnuts, cinnamon and 2 teaspoons sugar on waxed paper. Dip hot pastries in cold syrup. Remove with slotted spoon. Roll in walnut mixture to coat.

Constance Lebel
New Ipswich, New Hampshire

ALMOND TORTE BARS

1/2 c. butter, softened
1/2 c. sugar
2 egg yolks, beaten
1/4 tsp. almond extract
1 1/4 c. flour
1 tsp. baking powder
1/2 tsp. salt
1 c. packed dark brown sugar
1 egg white, stiffly beaten
Chopped nuts

Cream butter and sugar in bowl until light and fluffy. Add egg yolks, almond extract, 2 tablespoons warm water, flour, baking powder and salt; blend well. Spread in 7 x 11-inch baking pan. Fold brown sugar into egg white. Spread over dough. Sprinkle with nuts. Bake at 325 degrees for 30 minutes. Cut into bars.

Victoria Cummings
White Plains, New York

GOODIES

1 c. margarine, softened
1 c. cream-style cottage cheese
2 c. sifted flour
1 c. finely ground pecans
Corn syrup
3 doz. pecan halves

Combine margarine and cottage cheese in bowl; blend well. Mix in flour. Shape into ball. Chill for 1 hour or longer. Divide dough into thirds. Roll 1/8 inch thick on floured cloth. Cut into 3-inch squares. Mix pecans with 1/2 cup corn syrup in bowl. Place 1 teaspoon on each dough square. Fold in corners, overlapping in center. Dip pecan halves into corn syrup. Press into center of each pastry. Place on baking sheet. Bake at 350 degrees for 25 minutes.

Carole Curtis
Myrtle Beach, South Carolina

WENATCHEE APPLE BRAID

3 Washington State apples, peeled, quartered
1/2 c. finely chopped dried apricots
6 tbsp. broken walnuts
2 tbsp. brown sugar
1 tbsp. melted butter
2 tsp. shredded lemon rind
1 tsp. cinnamon
1 recipe 2-crust lemon pie pastry

WENATCHEE APPLE BRAID

Cook apples in 1/4 cup water in saucepan. Drain and measure 1 cup applesauce. Mix with apricots, walnuts, brown sugar, melted butter, lemon rind and cinnamon in bowl. Roll out pastry to 8 x 14-inch rectangle. Spoon apple mixture down center of pastry. Cut pastry 2 1/2 inches from both sides at 1-inch intervals. Fold strips alternately across top of filling. Moisten strips to secure at overlap point. Place on baking sheet. Bake at 425 degrees for 35 minutes or until golden brown. Garnish with cinnamon sugar or confectioners' sugar glaze.

Photograph for this recipe above.

BISCOCHITOS

1 lb. pure lard, softened
1 3/4 c. sugar
3 tsp. aniseed
4 egg yolks
7 c. flour
3 1/2 tsp. baking powder
1 tsp. salt
6 oz. orange juice
1 tsp. cinnamon

Cream lard and 1 1/4 cups sugar in bowl until fluffy. Beat in aniseed and egg yolks. Sift flour, baking powder and salt together. Add to creamed mixture alternately with orange juice, mixing well after each addition. Knead until smooth, dampening hands with warm water as necessary. Roll 1/4 inch thick on floured surface. Cut into 2 1/2-inch squares. Combine 1/2 cup sugar with cinnamon. Dip pastry in cinnamon mixture. Place on baking sheet. Bake at 350 degrees for 10 to 12 minutes or until light golden.

Concha Encinias
Santa Rosa, New Mexico

LOVE LETTERS

3/4 c. butter, softened
6 eggs, separated
3/4 c. flour
Pinch of salt
3/4 c. confectioners' sugar
3/4 c. ground walnuts
Cinnamon to taste

Cream butter in bowl. Stir in egg yolks then flour and salt. Chill, covered, overnight. Add confectioners' sugar to beaten egg whites gradually, beating until stiff. Fold in walnuts. Roll pastry into 22 thin squares on floured surface. Spoon filling onto pastry. Fold pastry into thirds then fold ends to center making a square. Place on baking sheet. Bake at 350 degrees for 25 minutes. Sprinkle with mixture of additional confectioners' sugar and cinnamon.

Betty Rowe
Santa Fe, New Mexico

SOUR CREAM PASTRIES

1 c. butter
2 1/2 c. flour
1 egg, beaten
1/2 c. sour cream
1/2 c. apricot preserves
1/2 c. coconut
1/4 c. chopped walnuts
1/4 c. sugar

Cut butter into flour in bowl until crumbly. Mix egg and sour cream in small bowl. Add to flour mixture; blend well. Chill dough for several hours. Divide into 4 equal portions. Roll into 10-inch circles on floured surface. Spread with preserves. Sprinkle with coconut and wal-

nuts. Cut each circle into 12 wedges. Roll into crescent shapes. Sprinkle with sugar. Place on baking sheet. Bake at 350 degrees for 20 minutes. Yield: 4 dozen.

Judy Myron
Washington, D. C.

SPICED DANISH BARS

Margarine
2 1/2 c. sifted flour
Salt
1 1/3 c. mincemeat
1 tsp. grated lemon rind
3 eggs
2 c. sifted confectioners' sugar
1/4 c. light cream
1 tsp. vanilla extract

Cut 1 stick margarine into 1 1/4 cups flour and 1/2 teaspoon salt in bowl until crumbly. Add 3 tablespoons cold water; stir until just blended. Press into 10 x 15-inch jelly roll pan. Spread mincemeat on top. Combine 1 stick margarine with 1 cup boiling water in saucepan. Bring to a boil. Stir in rind and 1 1/4 cups flour. Add eggs 1 at a time, beating well after each addition. Spread over mincemeat. Bake at 400 degrees for 35 to 40 minutes or until golden brown. Blend 1 tablespoon margarine, pinch of salt and remaining ingredients in bowl until smooth. Spread over pastry. Cut into bars.

Marty Stowers
Detroit, Michigan

DANISH DEERHORNS

1/2 c. butter, softened
1/2 c. sugar
4 eggs, beaten
2 c. sifted flour
Oil for deep frying
Confectioners' sugar

Cream butter and sugar in bowl. Add eggs; mix well. Add flour gradually; mix well. Chill for 1 hour. Roll on floured surface. Cut into triangles. Roll as for crescents. Deep-fry at 365 degrees until light brown. Drain on paper towel. Sprinkle with confectioners' sugar. Serve hot. Yield: 3 dozen.

Betty McMillan
Shaker Heights, Ohio

CANNOLI CICCOLATI

3 c. sifted flour
1 1/2 c. sugar
1 tsp. cinnamon
1/4 tsp. salt
3 tbsp. shortening
2 eggs, well beaten
2 tbsp. white vinegar
1 egg white, slightly beaten
Oil for deep frying
3 c. ricotta cheese
2 tsp. vanilla extract
1/4 c. cocoa
1 c. chopped toasted pecans
Confectioners' sugar

Sift flour, 1/4 cup sugar, cinnamon and salt into bowl. Cut in shortening. Stir in eggs; blend in vinegar and 2 tablespoons cold water, 1 tablespoon at a time. Knead on lightly floured surface for 5 to 8 minutes or until smooth. Wrap in waxed paper. Chill for 30 minutes. Roll dough 1/8 inch thick. Cut into 6 x 4 1/2-inch ovals. Wrap loosely around 6-inch lengths of heavy-duty aluminum foil, folded in 3 thicknesses and rolled to 1-inch diameter. Seal edges with egg white. Deep-fry in 360-degree oil until golden brown. Drain on paper towels. Cool slightly and remove foil. Cool completely. Combine cheese, vanilla, cocoa and remaining 1 1/4 cups sugar in blender container. Process until smooth. Add 1/2 cup pecans. Chill in refrigerator. Fill fried pastry with cheese mixture. Dip ends in remaining chopped pecans. Dust with confectioners' sugar. Serve immediately. Yield: 1 1/2 dozen.

CHOUX RIBBONS

Vanilla extract, rum or lemon juice to taste
1 recipe cream puff pastry (pg. 100)
Oil for deep frying
Sugar

Blend flavoring into cream puff pastry. Spoon into pastry tube. Pipe several strips at a time into deep 375-degree oil. Fry for 5 to 7 minutes or until golden brown. Drain on paper towels. Sprinkle with sugar.

Estelle Harmon
Pineola, Mississippi

FATTIGMANNS BAKKELSER

10 egg yolks
1/3 c. sugar
1/2 c. whipping cream
1 tbsp. Cognac
1 tsp. cardamom
1/2 tsp. grated lemon rind
2 to 2 1/2 c. flour
Oil for deep frying
Confectioners' sugar

Beat egg yolks with sugar in bowl for 10 minutes. Stir in cream, Cognac, cardamom, lemon rind and enough flour to make stiff dough. Chill, covered, for 3 hours or longer. Roll 1/16 to 1/8 inch thick on floured surface. Cut into 2 x 4-inch diamonds. Cut 1 inch horizontal slit in center of each. Draw long point of diamond through slit and fold back. Fry in hot deep oil for 15 seconds on each side or until light brown; drain. Store in airtight container. Sprinkle with confectioners' sugar just before serving. Yield: 4 dozen.

Camille Pincher
Charlotte, North Carolina

LOVE CAKES

12 egg yolks
1/2 tsp. salt
1 tbsp. (heaping) confectioners' sugar
1/2 c. sour cream
1 tbsp. melted butter
1/2 tsp. vanilla extract
1 1/2 oz. whiskey
Flour
Oil for deep frying

Beat egg yolks and salt until light. Add next 5 ingredients; mix well. Stir in enough flour to make medium-soft dough. Roll on floured surface into 8-inch rectangle. Cut into 2-inch strips. Make long slit in center of each strip. Pull one end through slit to make bow. Deep-fry in 350-degree oil until light brown, turning once. Drain on paper towels. Sprinkle with additional confectioners' sugar.

Virginia Lamore
Warren, Michigan

EQUIVALENT CHART

WHEN RECIPE CALLS FOR:	YOU NEED:
BREAD & CEREAL	
1 c. soft bread crumbs	2 slices
1 c. fine dry bread crumbs	4-5 slices
1 c. small bread cubes	2 slices
1 c. fine cracker crumbs	24 saltines
1 c. fine graham cracker crumbs	14 crackers
1 c. vanilla wafer crumbs	22 wafers
1 c. crushed corn flakes	3 c. uncrushed
4 c. cooked macaroni	1 8-oz. package
3 1/2 c. cooked rice	1 c. uncooked
DAIRY	
1 c. freshly grated cheese	1/4 lb.
1 c. cottage cheese or sour cream	1 8-oz. carton
2/3 c. evaporated milk	1 sm. can
1 2/3 c. evaporated milk	1 tall can
1 c. whipped cream	1/2 c. heavy cream
SWEET	
1 c. semisweet chocolate pieces	1 6-oz. package
2 c. granulated sugar	1 lb.
4 c. sifted confectioners' sugar	1 lb.
2 1/4 c. packed brown sugar	1 lb.
MEAT	
3 c. diced cooked meat	1 lb., cooked
2 c. ground cooked meat	1 lb., cooked
4 c. diced cooked chicken	1 5-lb. chicken
NUTS	
1 c. chopped nuts	4 oz. shelled
	1 lb. unshelled
VEGETABLES	
4 c. sliced or diced raw potatoes	4 medium
2 c. cooked green beans	1/2 lb. fresh or 1 16-oz. can
1 c. chopped onion	1 large
4 c. shredded cabbage	1 lb.
2 c. canned tomatoes	1 16-oz. can
1 c. grated carrot	1 large
2 1/2 c. lima beans or red beans	1 c. dried, cooked
1 4-oz. can mushrooms	1/2 lb. fresh
FRUIT	
4 c. sliced or chopped apples	4 medium
2 c. pitted cherries	4 c. unpitted
3 to 4 tbsp. lemon juice plus 1 tsp. grated peel	1 lemon
1/3 c. orange juice plus 2 tsp. grated peel	1 orange
1 c. mashed banana	3 medium
4 c. cranberries	1 lb.
3 c. shredded coconut	1/2 lb.
4 c. sliced peaches	8 medium
1 c. pitted dates or candied fruit	1 8-oz. package
2 c. pitted prunes	1 12-oz. package
3 c. raisins	1 15-oz. package

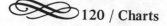

COMMON EQUIVALENTS

1 tbsp. = 3 tsp.	6 1/2 to 8-oz. can = 1 c.
2 tbsp. = 1 oz.	10 1/2 to 12-oz. can = 1 1/4 c.
4 tbsp. = 1/4 c.	14 to 16-oz. can (No. 300) = 1 3/4 c.
5 tbsp. + 1 tsp. = 1/3 c.	16 to 17-oz. can (No. 303) = 2 c.
8 tbsp. = 1/2 c.	1-lb. 4-oz. can or 1-pt. 2-oz. can (No. 2) = 2 1/2 c.
12 tbsp. = 3/4 c.	1-lb. 13-oz. can (No. 2 1/2) = 3 1/2 c.
16 tbsp. = 1 c.	3-lb. 3-oz. can or 46-oz. can or 1-qt. 14-oz. can =
1 c. = 8 oz. or 1/2 pt.	5 3/4 c.
4 c. = 1 qt.	6 1/2-lb. or 7-lb. 5-oz. can (No. 10) = 12 to 13 c.
4 qt. = 1 gal.	

METRIC CONVERSION CHART

VOLUME

1 tsp.	=	4.9 cc
1 tbsp.	=	14.7 cc
1/3 c.	=	28.9 cc
1/8 c.	=	29.5 cc
1/4 c.	=	59.1 cc
1/2 c.	=	118.3 cc
3/4 c.	=	177.5 cc
1 c.	=	236.7 cc
2 c.	=	473.4 cc
1 fl. oz.	=	29.5 cc
4 oz.	=	118.3 cc
8 oz.	=	236.7 cc

1 pt.	=	473.4 cc
1 qt.	=	.946 liters
1 gal.	=	3.7 liters

CONVERSION FACTORS

Liters	X	1.056	=	Liquid quarts
Quarts	X	0.946	=	Liters
Liters	X	0.264	=	Gallons
Gallons	X	3.785	=	Liters
Fluid ounces	X	29.563	=	Cubic centimeters
Cubic centimeters	X	0.034	=	Fluid ounces
Cups	X	236.575	=	Cubic centimeters
Tablespoons	X	14.797	=	Cubic centimeters
Teaspoons	X	4.932	=	Cubic centimeters
Bushels	X	0.352	=	Hectoliters
Hectoliters	X	2.837	=	Bushels

WEIGHT

1 dry oz.	=	28.3 Grams
1 lb.	=	.454 Kilograms

CONVERSION FACTORS:

Ounces (Avoir.)	X	28.349	=	Grams
Grams	X	0.035	=	Ounces
Pounds	X	0.454	=	Kilograms
Kilograms	X	2.205	=	Pounds

SUBSTITUTION CHART

	INSTEAD OF:	USE:
BAKING	1 tsp. baking powder 1 c. sifted all-purpose flour 1 c. sifted cake flour 1 tsp. cornstarch (for thickening)	1/4 tsp. soda plus 1/2 tsp. cream of tartar 1 c. plus 2 tbsp. sifted cake flour 1 c. minus 2 tbsp. sifted all-purpose flour 2 tbsp. flour or 1 tbsp. tapioca

SWEET	1 1-oz. square chocolate
	1 2/3 oz. semisweet
	    chocolate
	1 c. granulated sugar
	
	1 c. honey
		3 to 4 tbsp. cocoa plus 1 tsp. shortening
		1 oz. unsweetened chocolate plus 4 tsp. sugar
		
		1 c. packed brown sugar or 1 c. corn syrup,
		    molasses, honey minus 1/4 c. liquid
		1 to 1 1/4 c. sugar plus 1/4 c. liquid or
		    1 c. molasses or corn syrup

DAIRY	1 c. sweet milk 1 c. sour milk 1 c. buttermilk 1 c. light cream 1 c. heavy cream 1 c. sour cream	1 c. sour milk or buttermilk plus 1/2 tsp. soda 1 c. sweet milk plus 1 tbsp. vinegar or lemon juice of 1 c. buttermilk 1 c. sour milk or 1 c. yogurt 7/8 c. skim milk plus 3 tbsp. butter 3/4 c. skim milk plus 1/3 c. butter 7/8 c. sour milk plus 3 tbsp. butter
	1 c. bread crumbs	3/4 c. cracker crumbs

SEASONINGS	1 c. catsup
	
	1 tbsp. prepared mustard
	1 tsp. Italian spice
	
	1 tsp. allspice
	1 medium onion
	
	1 clove of garlic
	
	1 tsp. lemon juice
		1 c. tomato sauce plus 1/2 c. sugar
		    plus 2 tbsp. vinegar
		1 tsp. dry mustard
		1/4 tsp. each oregano, basil, thyme, rosemary
		    plus dash of cayenne
		1/2 tsp. cinnamon plus 1/8 tsp. cloves
		1 tbsp. dried minced onion or 1 tsp. onion
		    powder
		1/8 tsp. garlic powder or 1/8 tsp. instant
		    minced garlic or 3/4 tsp. garlic salt
		    or 5 drops of liquid garlic
		1/2 tsp. vinegar

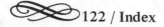

INDEX

PHOTOGRAPHY CREDITS

Cover: JELL-O Instant Pudding and Pie Filling; Filbert/Hazelnut Institute; The J. M. Smucker Company; California Apricot Advisory Board; United Fresh Fruit and Vegetable Association; Ruth Lundgren, Limited; Pie Filling Institute; Best Foods: Division of Corn Products Company; National Dairy Council; Armour and Company; Evaporated Milk Association; American Dry Milk Association; California Raisin Advisory Board; California Strawberry Advisory Board; Ocean Spray Cranberries; Washington State Apple Commission; and Processed Apple Institute.

FAVORITE RECIPES PRESS COOKBOOK ORDER FORM

TITLE	Item #	Qty.	Price	Total
Add Postage & Handling.	99929		$ 1.95	$ 1.95
		Subtotal		
		Add state & local tax		
		Total Payment		

**To place your charge card orders,
call our toll-free number
1-800-251-1542
or clip and mail convenient order form.**

Name _____

Address _____

City _____ State _____ Zip _____

Daytime Phone ( ) _____

☐ Payment enclosed.

☐ Please Charge My: ☐ MasterCard   ☐ Visa

Expiration Date _____

Account Number _____

Signature _____

- No COD orders please.
- Prices subject to change without notice.
- Books offered subject to availability.
- Make checks payable to Great American Opportunities.

Please mail completed order form to:
**Great American Opportunities, Inc.
P. O. Box 77, Nashville, TN 37202**